BORDERS

FOUNTAINHEAD PRESS V SERIES

Edited by
Isabel Baca

Series Editors
Lee Bauknight and Brooke Rollins

FOUNTAINHEAD
PRESS

Our green initiatives include:

Electronic Products
We deliver products in non-paper form whenever possible. This includes pdf downloadables, flash drives, & CDs.

Electronic Samples
We use Xample, a new electronic sampling system. Instructor samples are sent via a personalized web page that links to pdf downloads.

FSC Certified Printers
All of our printers are certified by the Forest Service Council which promotes environmentally and socially responsible management of the world's forests. This program allows consumer groups, individual consumers, and businesses to work together hand-in-hand to promote responsible use of the world's forests as a renewable and sustainable resource.

Recycled Paper
Most of our products are printed on a minimum of 30% post-consumer waste recycled paper.

Support of Green Causes
When we do print, we donate a portion of our revenue to green causes. Listed below are a few of the organizations that have received donations from Fountainhead Press. We welcome your feedback and suggestions for contributions, as we are always searching for worthy initiatives.
Rainforest 2 Reef
Environmental Working Group

Design by Susan Moore

Books may be purchased for educational purposes.

For information, please call or write:

1-800-586-0330

Fountainhead Press
Southlake, TX 76092

Web Site: www.fountainheadpress.com
E-mail: customerservice@fountainheadpress.com

First Edition

ISBN: 978-1-59871-472-9

Printed in the United States of America

INTRODUCTION TO THE FOUNTAINHEAD PRESS V SERIES

BY BROOKE ROLLINS AND LEE BAUKNIGHT
Series Editors

The *Fountainhead Press V Series* is a new collection of single-topic readers that take a unique look at some of today's most pressing issues. Designed to give writing students a more nuanced introduction to public discourse—on the environment, on food, and on digital life, to name a few of the topics—the books feature writing, research, and invention prompts that can be adapted to nearly any kind of college writing class. Each *V Series* textbook focuses on a single issue and includes multi-genre and multimodal readings and assignments that move the discourse beyond the most familiar patterns of debate—patterns usually fettered by entrenched positions and often obsessed with "winning."

The ultimate goal of the series is to help writing students—who tend to hover on the periphery of public discourse—think, explore, find their voices, and skillfully compose texts in a variety of media and genres. Not only do the books help students think about compelling issues and how they might address them, they also give students the practice they need to develop their research, rhetorical, and writing skills. Together, the readings, prompts, and longer assignments show students how to add their voices to the conversations about these issues in meaningful and productive ways.

With enough readings and composing tasks to sustain an entire quarter or semester, and inexpensive enough to be used in combination with other rhetorics and readers, the *Fountainhead Press V Series* provides instructors with the flexibility to build the writing courses they want and need to teach. An instructor interested in deeply exploring environmental issues, for example, could design a semester- or quarter-long course using *Green*, the first of the *V Series* texts. On the other hand, an instructor who wanted to teach discrete units on different issues could use two or more of the *V Series* books. In either case, the texts would give students ample opportunity—and a variety of ways—to engage with the issues at hand.

The *V Series* uses the term "composition" in its broadest sense. Of course, the textbooks provide students plenty of opportunities to write, but they also include assignments that take students beyond the page. Books in the series encourage students to explore other modes of communication by prompting them to design web sites, for example; to produce videos, posters, and presentations; to conduct primary and secondary research; and to develop projects with community partners that might incorporate any number of these skills. Ultimately, we have designed the *Fountainhead Press V Series* to work for teachers and students. With their carefully chosen readings, built-in flexibility, and sound rhetorical grounding, the *V Series* books would be a dynamic and user-friendly addition to any writing class.

TABLE OF CONTENTS

INTRODUCTION: CROSSING BORDERS

By Isabel Baca

I am a product of the U.S.-México border. I am a living example of one who has crossed—and continues to cross—borders. I was born in El Paso, Texas but lived the first years of my life in Juárez, Chihuahua, México. My parents, both born in México, taught me my mother tongue—Spanish. But early in my education, my father, seeking better job venues and better educational and professional opportunities for our family, moved us across the border to El Paso. I was placed in a grade school classroom knowing little to no English. My teacher knew no Spanish; my best friends became an African-American boy and a German girl, neither of whom knew any Spanish. We communicated through signs and facial expressions, especially when they looked at me with sadness and anger when our teacher would hit my hand with a ruler whenever she heard me speaking Spanish with Mexican-American classmates. What was I doing wrong? This was particularly confusing to me since she never gave me a reason for doing this, for penalizing me. To make this situation even more difficult to comprehend, I would go home and be ordered to only speak Spanish, since my mother knew little English and hated for us to forget our home language, Spanish. What was wrong with English if I was to use it at school? These clashing messages about my language paved the way to a self-discovery, a reflective, and critical journey. Who was I? Where did I belong? How and would I fit in? And so my journey began—a journey surrounded by borders which I had to cross and which pushed me to build bridges.

As I began working on this book, I debated on whether to focus on geographical borders or to give you, the reader, the opportunity to explore those physical, cultural, and emotional borders that you may see and experience in your daily life. Webster's New Universal Unabridged Dictionary defines "border" as "the extreme part or surrounding line; the confine or exterior limit of a country, or any region or track of land." Other dictionaries are more specific, defining "border" more narrowly, and two such definitions apply to this text: "Border" is "the line that separates one country, state, province, etc., from another; frontier line." It is also "**the** border between the U.S. and México, especially along the Rio Grande." Though *Borders* examines this geographical and physical area of the Southwest, of what is also known as *the borderland, la frontera*—a region that spans both the United States and México, it also explores borders dealing with much more than simply geography. *Borders* describes linguistic, cultural, and emotional borders, showing how crossing such borders may lead to opportunity and benefits and/or confusion, problems, and marginalization. Thus, *Borders* also addresses immigration issues on the U.S.-México border.

Clearly, then, *Borders* goes beyond the physical line or river that separates these two countries. It explores what Heewon Chang identifies as a "cultural border." Chang explains how a border is more than a demarcation line; it can denote power. Chang says, "[A border] is a symbol of power that imposes inclusion and exclusion. A cultural border connotes a barrier that a more powerful side constructs to guard its own political power, cultural knowledge and privileges."[1] In other words, a border can exist culturally, linguistically, politically, and can involve religion, gender, age, and other issues. For example, as someone who was born and lives on a border, I have experience living in this physical space, but my experience crosses several other borders that make me who I am—a true product of the U.S.-México border. Culture, language, politics, religion, and gender, among many other factors, build borders in communities, societies, nations, and the world.

Because I was born and live on the El Paso-Juárez border, I was fortunately exposed to both English and Spanish. I consider myself bilingual and bicultural. I have been exposed and brought up with both cultures existing on the border, which together comprise what has come to be known as "the border culture." People on the border can relate to both the 4th of July and 16

1 Change, Hewoon. "Re-examining the Rhetoric of the 'Cultural Border'." http://www.edchange.org/multicultural/papers/heewon.html

de Septiembre (September 16th)—independence days for the United States and México. People on the border can have fun playing Bingo and la loteria and hitting a piñata. People on the border hear different languages and dialects on a daily basis. They can communicate with more diverse people, celebrate more occasions, hold more festive days, and cherish an array of different customs, histories, and traditions. But this experience can cause conflicts for individuals, too, involving their identity, their literacy skills, their position in society, their "belonging" to one, or the other, or both sides of the border. The question then becomes: Do you want to cross borders? In crossing borders, what happens to your language, culture, beliefs, and life? What happens if you choose to build more bridges to connect these borders? Or what if you choose to not build bridges but more walls and fences to stop crossing borders?

Borders opens doors by having you reflect and analyze the different borders individuals can, want, or are forced to cross. *Borders* includes an array of reading selections focusing on different borders existing in daily life, particularly borders that individuals living in the Southwest may encounter. But you will quickly see how these borders can apply to any physical area connecting two parts, whether it is two nations, two cities, two neighborhoods, two workplaces, two institutions, or two entities of different sorts. Borders, remember, can also exist between languages, cultures, races, age groups, political and religious affiliations, and genders.

To help you better understand and think critically through the different issues surrounding borders and immigration, *Borders* includes diverse genres: poems, narratives, interviews, debates, cartoons, articles, reviews and letters. It presents both written and visual texts. *Borders* includes research, invention, and composing prompts and activities. As you read through these selections and complete the various exercises, projects, and assignments, you will be exposed to different views on borders and immigration. You will write essays, conduct interviews, give presentations, work collaboratively with classmates, participate in class and small group discussions, complete prewriting techniques such as researching and brainstorming, and even practice service-learning within your community.

My wish for you, the reader, is to not only practice writing, create documents, and critically analyze different literary genres, but to go beyond the learning that happens in a classroom. These readings will encourage you to think and reflect on the different borders existing in your life. They will push you to take a critical view of the borders, the crossing of borders that humans do to survive, to be heard, to be welcomed, to be noticed and recognized, or to change their lives. Ask yourself if you want to cross borders. How do you view those crossing borders? Why do you feel this way? How and when should you cross borders? Are you building bridges or fences and walls? When are bridges necessary? When are walls a must? Who should decide if you are allowed to cross specific borders? In answering these questions, you will need to examine the time, place, context, purpose, audience, and subject for each situation you are addressing. You will practice rhetorical techniques which will assist you in conveying your ideas and purpose.

To get you started, the following exercises introduce you to the concept of borders.

Examine this book's front cover. What do you see? What does this image say to you? Pablo Casals, a Spanish cellist and conductor, once said, "The love of one's country is a splendid thing. But why should love stop at the border?" How does this statement relate to the book's cover?

How is the cover image appropriate and effective for *Borders?* Or do you find it to be ineffective and/or inappropriate? Why? Is the image speaking of only one type of border? If so, which border? If you see more borders in the cover, what are these? Explain your answer by referring to specific points in the cover. Consider each item and figure in the cover: the flags, the couple, their closeness to each other, etc.

With one or two of your classmates, create, design, draw or find an alternate cover for this book. How does your group's selected image represent *Borders?* Which border is your image addressing? Show your image to the class and explain your selection in detail.

Write a narrative essay where you describe a personal border that you have had to cross in your life. This can be a physical, cultural, linguistic, or emotional border. Be sure to show how this is indeed a border. How did you or are you crossing this border? Was there a bridge connecting the two sides of this border? Or were you forced to build a bridge or enter the other side of the border without permission, just making your way across to the other side? What did you leave behind? What did you find on the other side? Why was it or is it important for you to cross this border? Describe this border and your experience in detail. Allow the reader to live through your experience of crossing this border.

BORDERS

Beatriz Terrazas, with a B.A. in journalism, has worked both as a writer and photographer for the Fort Worth Star Telegram *and* The Dallas Morning News. *She is a freelancer in Dallas, TX.*

THE RIVER THAT RUNS THROUGH ME

BY BEATRIZ TERRAZAS

I miss the Rio Grande. In my mind I see it, and I smell menudo spiced with oregano. I see it and I hear the clop of horses' hoofs outside my grandfather's house in Juárez, feel the beat of a corridor lifting my feet.

I've been away from El Paso/Juárez for 20 years now, but I still call it home. Early this year, driving along Interstate 10, I caught a glimpse of the Rio Grande. The river lay there between the two cities where I grew up, dry and bare in spots, looking more like a snake that had slithered up to the wrong end of a farmer's hoe than the mighty force implied by its name. It lay there, broken, totally passable for anyone wishing to cross it either north or south but for the white border patrol vehicles planted like sentinels along it.

The river—and all it stands for to me—has become invisible despite being in the background of our daily political discourse. I read or hear story after story about international border fences in

The Rio Grande, to the right, is the United States, to the left is México

Texas: The town of McAllen agreed to reinforce its flood walls rather than submit to new fencing to deter trespassers. A federal judge ordered Eagle Pass to surrender more than 200 acres of land for fence construction.

I keep hoping others will see what I see: not borders and fences and illegal immigrants but the Rio Grande itself. To those of us who love it, the river is not merely a boundary of México, it's a living thing. And to those of us who carry it in our veins, it is the story of our lives. The river haunts me. Several years ago, I traveled long stretches of the Rio Grande from its headwaters in Colorado to its mouth in South Texas. Meeting others along its trajectory was a lesson in how this bony, nearly 1,900-mile channel has shaped and influenced people. I came to see how the river is irrevocably intertwined with the child I was, the woman I am. It tethers my soul to the arid landscape in West Texas, and to México. But today's Rio Grande is oh so different from the river I once knew.

The river of my youth flowed deep and strong near Las Cruces, N.M., where my family used to picnic. Once, when I was 6 or 7, my mother commanded my siblings and me to stay on the bank and wait for our father before jumping in to play. While he unloaded sandwiches and chips from the trunk, she stepped into the water for a quick swim. Then she was shouting and in just seconds her voice sounded far away and she looked tiny, her arm a matchstick floating on the water. She was drowning! I shouted to my father: "Mi mami se está ahogando!" My father, all white skin and plaid trunks, leaped into the water, but by the time he reached her, she was standing on a sandbar. Later, she told us that la corriente, the current, swift and unseen beneath the river's surface had carried her away from us, but shhhh, it's okay now.

Another memory: I was about 10 and in Juárez playing quinceañera with my cousins on a packed-earth patio. We dreamed about that first dance and the white pearly dress like an upside-down tulip that would signal our passage to womanhood. We shuffled our feet to the song we sang aloud, our budding hips bending to the feat of the cumbia: "Ven a bailar quinceañera. Ven a gozar quinceañera." And though we couldn't see the river, as dusk fell, coloring the neighborhood purple and gray, its ghosts beckoned us. *You know La Llorona drowned her children in the river. You know that, right? Now she wanders the river crying, looking for other children, so watch out!*

In high school, some Latino boys threatened to throw into the river a white kid one of my friends was dating. Looking back, I wonder: Were they thinking of the deep symbolism of drowning a white boy in the waters that embodied their different ethnic histories? Probably not; they were just angry, disenfranchised in the way that brown-skinned boys were then, looking for a way to vent their feelings.

But what some people fail to understand—about me, about those boys—is that for us the river wasn't a barrier. An inconvenience, perhaps, when we had to cross the international bridge to visit our abuelas and primos or wait in long lines of chugging, overheated cars on the way back to our American lives. But the river was our connection, a witness to our attempts at straddling two cultures—to the fact that we could learn U.S. history in school during the week and spend Saturday nights celebrating weddings al otro lado. To the struggles of navigating two languages, two collective histories, and finding that with the passage of time, we were completely at home in neither one nor the other.

That's why seeing the disappearing Rio Grande fills me with such longing. I see it and taste the cinnamon coffee of mornings in my grandmother's kitchen. I see it and feel the sweat trickle down my back on a hot day, while my grandfather is lowered to his final resting place in a dusty cemetery. I see it and hear it calling my name as only a loved one can. It is the mirror that reflects the middle space between cultures and countries where I spent my formative years. Yet, for several months out of the year, even Google Earth would be hard-pressed to find this river between El Paso and, say, Presidio. During the summer it is dammed upstream for irrigation, its flow so greatly compromised that it dries up in some places and disappears.

The river seems to be vanishing just as I've realized I can't live without it. I worry that for all of our border talk, we are so blinded by political and economic issues that we don't really see the Rio Grande. I worry that we won't be able to control the invasive salt cedar breaking up its banks. I worry that we will divert its waters to the point of no return.

What happens then? La Llorona, the restless spirit whose existence calls for water, will have a rough time calling forth a chill by a dry channel. As for me, would losing the river mean losing a part of myself? Sunday picnics, high school raft races, crossing into México to watch my grandfather die—would all the memories dry up as well? I hope and pray the river outlives my family as the natural world is supposed to do.

And if I'm lucky, The Rio Grande will have been the great witness I think it is and will have carried the bones of my memories to be cradled in the sea.

Terrazas refers to "La Llorona" twice in her text. A popular legend in México, La Llorona is a story describing a beautiful woman who drowns her children in order to be with the man she loves. What is the significance of this reference in Terrazas' view of the Rio Grande? Research the story of "La Llorona" and relate it to Terrazas' experience.

In small groups, discuss how the Rio Grande represents the story of Terrazas' life and simultaneously how the river haunts her. Be prepared to explain your group's responses to your classmates.

Create a list showing how Terrazas belonged to each side of the river, of the U.S.-México border, ultimately making her feel that she was not home on either side of the border.

Norma E. Cantú is a native of the borderlands. She is an Associate Professor of English at Laredo State University and has published poetry, short fiction, and critical analyses. In this piece, Cantú explores the emotions of those living on the U.S.-México border, where she believes cultures both clash and unite.

LIVING ON THE BORDER: A WOUND THAT WILL NOT HEAL

By Norma E. Cantú

… The pain and joy of the borderlands—perhaps no greater or lesser than the emotions stirred by living anywhere contradictions abound, cultures clash and meld, and life is lived on an edge—come from a wound that will not heal and yet is forever healing. These lands have always been here; the river of people has flowed for centuries. It is only the designation "border" that is relatively new, and along with the term comes the life one lives in this "in between world" that makes us the "other," the marginalized . . .

—Norma E. Cantú

Living in the geographical area where the United States and México meet, the truth is always present. It gnaws at one's consciousness like a fear of rabid dogs and coyotes. Beneath every action lies the context of border life. And one must see that undergirding for what it is: the pain and sorrow of daily reminders that here disease runs rampant, here drug crimes take a daily toll, here infant mortality rates run as high or higher than those in third-world countries, here one cannot drink the water, and here, this land that is our land—and has been our land for generations—is not really ours. But one must also see border life in the context of its joys, its continuous healing, and its celebration of a life and culture that survives against all odds. For to do otherwise condemns us to falling into the vortex of pessimism and anomie where so many already dwell.

La frontera: the frontier, the edges, the limits, the boundaries, the borders, the cultures, the languages, the foods; but more than that, the unity and disunity: es lo mismo y no lo es (it's the same and it isn't). Chicana novelist Gloria Anzaldúa speaks of this same terrain, this same geography, but her words are hers; they are not mine, not ours, not those of everyone living along the border. However similar experiences may be, they are not the same, for the frontera is as varied as the geography from Matamoros/Brownsville to Tijuana/San Ysidro, and the people that inhabit this wrinkle in space are as varied as the indigenous peoples that first crossed it centuries ago and the peoples who continue to traverse it today. The Aztec pantheon didn't really rule these northern lands, and the norteno personality, customs, rites, and language are testament to that other native culture, now all but gone, which survives in vestiges sometimes as vague as an image in the sand, on the wall of a cave, or in the lexicon and intonation of a border native's speech.

These lands have always harbored transients, people moving sometimes north, sometimes south. Like birds making their annual trek, migrant workers board up their homes and pack things in trucks, and off they go with the local priest's blessing. In Laredo, in Eagle Pass, and elsewhere, the matachines celebrate on May 3, December 12, or another significant date, and as they congregate to dance in honor of the holy cross, the Virgen de Guadalupe, or other local devotions, they remember other lands and other times. Spanish and English languages both change along the border: Manachis are flour tortilla tacos in Laredo and Nuevo Laredo and within a fifty-mile radius of the area; the "calo" (slang) of the "batos locos," lowriders, "cholos," or "pachucos" maintains its literary quality in its excessive use of metaphor all along the stretch, yet changes from community to community, just as the names for food and even the foods themselves, change. Differences have been there since the settlement of the borderlands in the seventeenth and eighteenth centuries, and the changes brought upon the border culture have occurred over the span of more than three hundred years; yet there are other changes as well, ongoing changes that will alter the very fabric of borderlands culture.

The collusion of a myriad of cultures, not just Mexican and U.S., makes the borderlands unique. It is a culture forever in transition, changing visibly from year to year. The population increases in number and in variety, as Koreans, Indians, and other peoples of non-European, non-indigenous, and non-Mestizo origin flow into the region. Because of such an influx, it also changes environmentally, economically, and even in style.

The names for the river may be different—Rio Bravo/Rio Grande—but it's the same river whose life-giving waters flow down from Colorado, and whose life-taking waters spill out into the Gulf of México. The same river is a political boundary between two nation-states, but people on both sides of the river retain the customs of the settlers from Spain and from central México along with those of the original inhabitants, which they have inherited and adapted to their particular needs.

Newcomers integrate their ways into the existing culture, but the old ones remain. Intriguing syncretisms occur. Weddings, for example, integrate traditional "Mexican" customs such as the Arabic arras (marriage coins) and the Native lazo (bonding cord) along with the German-style polka or conjunto music and brindis (toast). An infant's baptism becomes an occasion for godparents to exchange prayers, an indigenous form encapsulated in a European logic. Conversely, a "quinceañera" (young woman's fifteenth birthday) becomes the modern-day puberty rite of a community. In local dance halls, dancers engage in weekly rites as culturally choreographed as those of the Catholic pilgrimages to santuarios from California to Texas; both customs embody forms and values that endure from times before European contact.

Gloria Anzaldúa says that "The U.S.-Mexican border es una herida abierta (is an open wound) where the third world grates against the first and bleeds" (Anzaldúa 1987). And she continues the metaphor by adding that before the wound heals it "hemorrhages again, the lifeblood of two worlds merging to form a third country, a border culture." First shaped by the signing of the Treaty of Guadalupe Hidalgo that cut the area in two, the wound has continuously bled, as politics, economics, and most recently environmental pollution exacerbate the laceration. If some healing occurs and a scab barely forms, a new blow strikes, such as the economic blow struck by the 1982 Mexican devaluation.

Ours is a history of conflict and resolution, of growth and devastation, of battles won and lost in conflicts not always of our making. Often these contradictory outcomes issue from the same set of historical events, like the development of the maquiladora industry, which provides jobs even as it renders the river's waters "a veritable cesspool" (*The Laredo Morning Times*, 1993). The inhabitants of the borderlands live in the consequences of this history, in the bleeding that never stops. Those of us who inhabit this land must live with daily human rights violations, contrasting world views, two forms of currency, and different "ways of doing things" that in some cases make life easier but in others nearly intolerable.

Immigration and emigration have shaped the borderlands. The exodus of Texas border natives to the metropolitan areas of Houston, Dallas, and San Antonio or to California or the Midwest during the 1950s was due in large measure to the depressed local economy. But, as immigration to the north occurred, emigration from México into the area continued. The unemployment rates often hovered around the teens and did not noticeably decrease, in spite of large numbers of families relocating elsewhere, settling out of the migrant labor stream in industrialized areas such as Chicago or going to work in other areas of Texas.

In the 1980s and 1990s, some of these same people, now retiring from steel mills in Illinois or factories in Detroit, returned as retirees and settled in the South Texas border communities they moved from forty years ago. For many, like my mother's cousins who moved away and worked for Bethlehem Steel, Christmas and summer vacation were times to visit relatives on the border; these days, it is their children who make the trip down south to visit them.

But in many cases the move was permanent. With little to come back to, families settled permanently in places like California, Wisconsin, and Nebraska. This was the experience of my father's cousin who lives in Omaha and who retired from the upholstering business she worked in for more than thirty years. She speaks of her life away and her reasons for leaving with great pain: There were no jobs to be had, political machines controlled the few jobs there were, the pay was below the national minimum wage, the schools were not good for their kids, and the streets weren't paved. At least up north, in spite of discrimination, language barriers, alien foods, and cold weather, there were jobs; one could dream of a better life. The border population is in transition once again as it has been for centuries. The healing occurs for but a short time when the newly formed scab is torn by a new element and the process begins anew.

The border is not homogeneous in geography or in culture; there are many borders, resplendent in their heterogeneity. We who live in these realities celebrate our day-to-day life with family "carne asada" gatherings; with civic events such as George Washington's birthday celebration with its numerous border icons like the abrazo (embracing) ceremony and the international parade; with high school graduations (currently attained by around fifty-five percent of students) and other markers of academic achievement; and with religious events, such as the matachines dance or the annual visit to the city by the image of the Virgen de San Juan de los Lagos in México, venerated on both sides of the border.

The pain and joy of the borderlands—perhaps no greater or lesser than the emotions stirred by living anywhere contradictions abound, cultures clash and meld, and life is lived on an edge—come from a wound that will not heal and yet is forever healing. These lands have always been here; the river of people has flowed for centuries. It is only the designation "border" that is relatively new, and along with the term comes the life one lives in this "in-between world" that makes us the "other," the marginalized. But, from our perspective, the "other" is outside, away from, and alien to, the border. This is our reality, and we, especially we Chicanos and Chicanas, negotiate it in our daily lives, as we contend with being treated as aliens ourselves. This in essence is the greatest wound: the constant reminder of our otherness.

REFERENCES

Anzaldúa, Gloria. *Borderlands/La Frontera: The New Mestiza.* San Francisco: Spinster/Aunt Lute Press, 1987.

"Rio Grande Labeled 'Virtual Cesspool.'" *The Laredo Morning Times,* 21 April 1993.

Based on Cantú's piece, list the different type of changes that have occurred in the borderlands. In other words, explain why the borderlands culture is "forever in transition." Give specific examples in your response.

Describe an instance when you felt like "the other," "the marginalized." Why did you feel this way? What were the circumstances? Do you think you have ever made someone feel marginalized? Explain.

In small groups, define and describe "different syncretisms" that occur on the borderlands? Which ones stand out the most in your mind? Have one member from the group report to the class what syncretism(s) are more vivid and present in the article according to your group.

Nate Blakeslee is a writer for Texas Monthly. In this article, Blakeslee explores immigration reform and the problem it poses for the Republican Party in Texas. He, too, addresses the political challenges surrounding immigration law reform in Texas and in the U.S.

BUSINESS AS USUAL

By Nate Blakeslee

Republicans in Texas have promised to pass strict immigration laws in the upcoming legislative session. They could do it—if the same old powerful interests within their own party weren't standing in their way.

—Nate Blakeslee

One morning in early September, I drove through Tyler with state representative Leo Berman looking for undocumented immigrants. About half a mile east of downtown, we found a group of perhaps ten or twelve men sitting under a small hackberry on a grassy hillside in front of a doughnut shop. "Here's the illegals right here," Berman said. "If you'd been here about three hours ago"—when contractors and foremen cruised by in their pickups, searching for day laborers—"you'd have seen a mass of people." These few stragglers in blue jeans and ball caps were the overlooked or unlucky, or maybe just the late sleepers. In recent years this corner has become the hub of a growing community of immigrants living in the northeast part of town. Berman pointed out the bright-orange facade of La Michoacana Meat Market across the street and a newly opened Mexican bakery nearby. "Michoacana" refers to a person or thing from Michoacán, a state in southwestern México. But in Texas, where the chain now has more than one hundred stores, it might as well mean "immigrants live here," since the company chooses its locations using census data to find pockets of Spanish speakers. Tyler, with a population of about 100,000 residents, got its store about eight years ago.

Berman, a 75-year-old retired Army lieutenant colonel who grew up in New York and has represented Tyler for twelve years, said his constituents are fed up. "If you take away the economy, it's the number one issue," he said. Berman's list of the evils of illegal immigration—the burden on taxpayers, the loss of jobs, and the threat of disease, crime, and drugs—will be familiar to anyone who has heard the Republican talking points on the failure of the Obama administration to secure our southern border. Less familiar is his take on who is standing in the way of the kind of tough response conservatives crave. "What people don't understand is that it's not just Democrats," he told me. "It's Republicans too." Chief among them, according to Berman, is Speaker of the House Joe Straus. Berman blames Straus, who is from San Antonio, for bottling up the dozen or so immigration bills he filed last session, which would have, among other things, prevented the children of undocumented immigrants from obtaining birth certificates, made it a state crime to transport or conceal an undocumented immigrant, and required undocumented immigrants to live in so-called sanctuary cities—a thumb in the eye to city councils that forbid discrimination based on the immigration status of their residents. Not one of the proposals was even allowed a vote on the House floor. Though Straus denies it, Berman is convinced that he made a deal with House Democrats who supported him for Speaker: No immigration bills would see the light of day. "He sold us out," he said. Berman, whose outspokenness on immigration has made him a champion of tea party conservatives, has announced his own candidacy for Speaker for the session that begins in January.

Even if House conservatives do manage to oust Straus, however, that won't alter the deeper and more fundamental problem that immigration reform poses for the Republican party in Texas. Many of the party's biggest funders, like Houston homebuilder Bob Perry, are captains of industries that employ huge numbers of recent immigrants, some with papers and some without. More than 40 percent of the roughly one million construction workers in Texas are immigrants from Latin America, so it stands to reason that Perry Homes, which builds thousands of houses a year in subdivisions across the state, is one of the largest employers of foreign-born workers in Texas. Perry is also the single biggest donor to Republican politicians and causes in Texas, including $380,000 to Governor Rick Perry and $335,000 to Lieutenant Governor David Dewhurst during the 2006 general election. Equally influential in Republican circles are prominent homebuilders David Weekley and his brother Richard, a founder of Texans for Lawsuit Reform, one of the most active PACs in state politics for the past ten years. Then there is Bo Pilgrim, whose chicken-processing empire is built in large part on foreign-born workers as well. Republican candidates for statewide office in Texas don't launch campaigns without first making a visit to these four men, and no immigration bill ever escapes the attention of their lobbyists in Austin.

"I don't care what Bob Perry or Bo Pilgrim has to say," Berman said. "My constituents sent me to Austin to do the right thing." What his constituents want, Berman says, is something that resembles Arizona's controversial Senate Bill 1070, which directs local law enforcement officers to check the immigration status of anyone they suspect of being in the country illegally, a duty generally reserved for federal immigration agents. That worries the powers that be in the Republican party. It's not just the disruption that a major fight over immigration would mean for the next session of the Legislature, where battles over budget cuts and redistricting are already looming. It's also the prospect of the state's biggest Republican donors squaring off against the party's grass roots.

"That kind of issue is so disruptive to so many people on so many levels," said Bill Miller, who is a principal at HillCo Partners, one of the most influential lobbying firms in the state and a frequent conduit for Bob Perry's political donations. "It's just not a good thing, and the few people who believe it is don't have anyone's interests at heart except their own."

But the fight is going to happen, and it will get ugly, especially if an Arizona-style bill comes to the floor of the Senate, where voting rules have traditionally made it easy to quietly kill controversial bills. In late July, Houston senator Dan Patrick created a stir when he all but promised, in the course of a televised debate with Democratic senator Mario Gallegos, that the Republicans would override the Senate's hallowed two-thirds voting rule—which requires two thirds of the members of that chamber to agree to debate a measure—to ram such a bill past the Democratic minority. One thing is for sure: When Berman and Patrick make their respective moves next session, Democrats may prove to be the least of their worries.

The national debate over illegal immigration has become so polarized that it's hard to remember how close the country came to making genuine progress on the issue only a few short years ago. In 2006 Bob Perry, Bo Pilgrim, and a host of other industry leaders and prominent Republicans from Texas and around the nation lined up behind President George W. Bush's effort to pass comprehensive immigration reform in Washington. "Neither the immigrants here today nor those we will need in the future should have to live in the shadows," read a *Dallas Morning News* opinion piece signed by Perry and his fellow Republicans. "These are good people with good values doing work that we need done, reaching for the American Dream and helping make it a reality for all." Bush's proposal had something for everyone: increased border security for conservatives, a path to citizenship for undocumented workers already here, and an assurance of a steady labor supply for employers. Karl Rove toured the country to gin up support for the package, stopping in, among other places, Tyler, where he was joined by U.S. senator John Cornyn and several of the city's largest employers, who endorsed the bill.

But that seems as long ago as the fabled "permanent Republican majority." Bush's effort foundered amid a rising tide of anti-immigrant sentiment bubbling up from the heartland—an organic, grassroots phenomenon that even Rove's legendary political acumen failed to anticipate. With the emergence of the Tea Party movement, stopping illegal immigration (along with fighting taxes and reducing the size of government) has now become a central organizing principle for conservatives, one so powerful that even state-level politicians, who have no real say over the nation's immigration policy, are compelled to offer at least some sort of legislative solution, however constitutionally dubious it may be. According to a tally by the National Conference of State Legislatures, 1,374 bills and resolutions dealing with immigration and refugees were introduced nationwide in the first six months of 2010. Arizona-type bills have been introduced in 22 states. In one sense it's an unlikely time for the issue to catch fire: Illegal immigration has dropped dramatically since the recession began, in 2008. Declining birth rates in México, meanwhile, have demographers predicting that we have already seen a peak in northern migration and that American employers may be facing labor shortages in twenty years.

Republicans in Washington can't decide if the groundswell is a good or bad thing. They have been happy enough to hang the porous border around President Obama's neck, hoping to ride the anti-immigrant wave to a new Republican majority in one or both chambers of Congress. Yet Rove, who has been telling anyone who will listen that the Arizona solution is bad for the Republican party's long-term prospects, has found himself labeled an "establishment" Republican, a dirty word in the Tea Party era. "There is an anti-immigrant tidal wave crashing through the Republican party," said state senator Eliot Shapleigh, an El Paso Democrat who for the past two sessions has led an informal working group—which includes some moderate Republicans—to track and defeat punitive immigration legislation. "I don't know how a Republican elected official can stand against it."

Carrollton Republican Burt Solomons very nearly drowned in that tidal wave last spring. Berman had blamed Solomons, a loyal Straus lieutenant, for bottling up his immigration bills in the State Affairs Committee, which he chaired last session. In the Republican primary, Tea Party conservatives backed Michael Murphy, a 37-year-old political consultant, to run against him, and he attacked Solomons on the immigration issue. Murphy came within a hair of ousting the sixteen-year incumbent. Murphy's campaign was funded largely by Peter Morrison, a real estate developer who sat on the local school board in Lumberton, near Beaumont. Morrison publishes a conservative newsletter that has become widely read among a network of Tea Party–type groups across the state. After Morrison and fellow conservative David Barton, a former vice chairman of the Republican Party of Texas, urged their followers to get behind Berman's Speaker bid, members of the House were inundated with faxes vilifying Straus. "People started calling me, saying, 'Make it stop,'" Berman gleefully told me. "I don't think Speaker Straus is going to be around much longer."

Not surprisingly, Solomons tells the story a different way. "Leo Berman is a liar," he said. "He couldn't pass his immigration bills under [former House Speaker Tom] Craddick either. He makes up conspiracy theories to explain his own failures. The fact is, we had a uniquely divided House last session, and we could hardly get anything done." Solomons seemed chastised by his brush with early retirement, however, and sounded more than convinced that this session was the time for tough action on immigration. "I think the lesson of the primary for me is that the electorate wants something done," he said. He didn't have much sympathy, he told me, for the arguments of homebuilders and growers who complain that rash action might kill the golden goose for the Texas economy. "Are they admitting that they can't run their businesses legally?" he said.

Bob Perry declined to comment for this story, as did Bo Pilgrim and several other high-profile Republican donors. In fact, the voice of industry in Texas has been conspicuously silent, even as the issue has come to dominate the election season. "We're monitoring the situation, but we have yet to gear up," said Bill

Hammond, the president of the Texas Association of Business. His take on the Arizona bill is the same as his position on state laws imposing sanctions on employers who hire undocumented workers: "We think it's misguided for Texas to step in. It's a federal problem that requires a federal solution." The real turning point, according to Hammond, will come early in the session, when Patrick makes his move in the Senate, which is the ultimate hurdle for any immigration bill because of the power of the Democratic minority. If Patrick fails to get the two-thirds rule suspended, Hammond can rest easy. But if he manages to get a bill to the floor, then the gloves will have to come off. Bill Miller said the party's big moneymen were watching closely, however quiet they may seem. "If they see this thing getting any traction," he said, "they'll pick up the phone and they'll make it unmistakable where they're coming from on this issue, which is, Are you guys out of your mind?"

When people talk about immigration in a place like Tyler, they are often talking about race, though they may not want to admit it. In the halls of the Legislature, however, the subtext of the immigration debate more often than not is wages. What the business community knows is that the face of manual labor is changing: Nationwide, 47 percent of jobholders without high school diplomas are immigrants, up from 28 percent in 1993. Spanish is now the language spoken on construction sites, and large-scale agriculture has always relied on a steady supply of migrant workers, at least half of whom are believed to be undocumented. Hammond's constituents fear that any decrease in the size of the labor pool in Texas will eventually lead to rising wages, which is why the only acceptable outcome of immigration reform from the industry perspective is one in which the estimated 10 million to 12 million undocumented immigrants remain in the country under some legal aegis.

Organized labor in Texas supports this approach too, because the AFL-CIO can't organize workers who are not here legally, and it sees low union membership as the real reason Texas wages remain stagnant, not immigration. Ed Sills, the communications director for the Texas AFL-CIO, said he considers himself to be on Hammond's side in the fight. Still, he thinks Hammond and company are making a critical mistake by staying quiet and ceding the stage to the wing of the party represented by Berman. "They think they can get a short-term gain by letting the tea party forces dominate the discussion before the election," he said. Then, after voter anger over immigration leads to anticipated Republican gains in November, they can worry about tamping down expectations for any major initiatives after the legislative session starts.

But once the genie has been let out of the bottle, who will do the hard and painful work necessary to get it back in? "I think there will be a price to pay," Sills said. What happens, for example, if an Arizona-type bill does land on Rick Perry's desk? Perry has skillfully deflected efforts to pin him down on this question, suggesting that an Arizona law is "not right" for Texas but not definitively saying he will veto it. Given that Texas will have a Hispanic majority as early as 2020, his misgivings are not hard to understand—what would it mean for the party's future prospects if he signs it? "I think it would mean a serious setback of long duration," Miller said. "If you want to do it and kill yourself, go right ahead. If you want to commit suicide, you know, pull the trigger."

For now, the person with his finger on the trigger is Dan Patrick. In an interview at his Capitol office, Patrick, whose popular talk radio show has made him a standard-bearer for the party's right wing, nevertheless took pains to distance himself from bomb throwers like Berman, who made national headlines when he called Obama "God's punishment" on America at a rally last spring, or Berman's House colleague Debbie Riddle, who infamously engaged Anderson Cooper in a discussion of "terror babies" on national TV. "I think I have shown that I am someone who can build a coalition and get bills passed," Patrick said. But he is also someone who is not afraid to put his fellow Republicans on the spot. "The one thing that I would remind every Republican who serves in the Legislature is that 2012 is not far away, and the Tea Party, which I think is the best thing that has happened in my lifetime, is not going away, and this issue sure as heck is not going away," Patrick said. "So if Republicans think, in the House or the Senate, that they can leave here next summer and go back to the voters in 2012 and say, 'You know, we had the majority of the House by about ten or twelve votes, and we had the majority of the Senate by seven or eight senators, and we still couldn't do anything about illegal immigration,' then I think some of those Republicans are going to have some explaining to do."

"They can't just say, 'Bob Perry wouldn't let me'?" I asked.

Patrick was uncharacteristically tongue-tied, considering, perhaps, not just the prospects of his party but his own political future as well. "The bottom line," he said finally, "is that there are no excuses."

Research Arizona's Senate Bill 1070. What is this bill proposing? How would it affect Arizona's residents? Research President George W. Bush's proposal on immigration. What is it proposing? What are its strengths? What are its weaknesses? Of the two, the bill and the proposal, which one do you think is more helpful and just? Why? How is President Bush's proposal similar or different to President Obama's plan for immigration reform?

As a class, divide yourselves into teams. Each team will examine the different sides to immigration. How is immigration helpful to the U.S.? How is immigration a problem? Be prepared, as a team, to give an overview of your team's evaluation of immigration in this country.

In a letter to your U.S. senator, present your position on immigration as an employer. Be clear on your stand. Describe how your position affects the labor pool in your state. Explain how, in your view, immigration plays a role in your hiring practices.

In this speech, President Barack Obama addresses the nation on the issue of immigration reform. Being his first speech on this topic, it describes Obama's initiative and efforts up to this point in his presidency. This speech took place on July 1, 2010 at the American University School of International Service in Washington, D.C.

REMARKS BY THE PRESIDENT ON COMPREHENSIVE IMMIGRATION REFORM

By President Barack Obama

THE PRESIDENT: Thank you very much. Thank you. Thank you. (Applause.) Everyone please have a seat. Thank you very much. Let me thank Pastor Hybels from near my hometown in Chicago, who took time off his vacation to be here today. We are blessed to have him.

I want to thank President Neil Kerwin and our hosts here at American University; acknowledge my outstanding Secretary of Labor, Hilda Solis, and members of my administration; all the members of Congress—Hilda deserves applause. (Applause.) To all the members of Congress, the elected officials, faith and law enforcement, labor, business leaders and immigration advocates who are here today—thank you for your presence.

I want to thank American University for welcoming me to the campus once again. Some may recall that the last time I was here I was joined by a dear friend, and a giant of American politics, Senator Edward Kennedy. (Applause.)

Teddy's not here right now, but his legacy of civil rights and health care and worker protections is still with us.

I was a candidate for President that day, and some may recall I argued that our country had reached a tipping point; that after years in which we had deferred our most pressing problems, and too often yielded to the politics of the moment, we now faced a choice: We could squarely confront our challenges with honesty and determination, or we could consign ourselves and our children to a future less prosperous and less secure.

I believed that then and I believe it now. And that's why, even as we've tackled the most severe economic crisis since the Great Depression, even as we've wound down the war in Iraq and refocused our efforts in Afghanistan, my administration has refused to ignore some of the fundamental challenges facing this generation.

We launched the most aggressive education reforms in decades, so that our children can gain the knowledge and skills they need to compete in a 21st century global economy.

We have finally delivered on the promise of health reform—reform that will bring greater security to every American, and that will rein in the skyrocketing costs that threaten families, businesses and the prosperity of our nation.

We're on the verge of reforming an outdated and ineffective set of rules governing Wall Street—to give greater power to consumers and prevent the reckless financial speculation that led to this severe recession.

And we're accelerating the transition to a clean energy economy by significantly raising the fuel-efficiency standards of cars and trucks, and by doubling our use of renewable energies like wind and solar power—steps that have the potential to create whole new industries and hundreds of thousands of new jobs in America.

So, despite the forces of the status quo, despite the polarization and the frequent pettiness of our politics, we are confronting the great challenges of our times. And while this work isn't easy, and the changes we seek won't always happen overnight, what we've made clear is that this administration will not just kick the can down the road.

Immigration reform is no exception. In recent days, the issue of immigration has become once more a source of fresh contention in our country, with the passage of a controversial law in Arizona and the heated reactions we've seen across America. Some have rallied behind this new policy. Others have protested and launched boycotts of the state. And everywhere, people have expressed frustration with a system that seems fundamentally broken.

Of course, the tensions around immigration are not new. On the one hand, we've always defined ourselves as a nation of immigrants—a nation that welcomes those willing to embrace America's precepts. Indeed, it is this constant flow of immigrants that helped to make America what it is. The scientific breakthroughs of Albert Einstein, the inventions of Nikola Tesla, the great ventures of Andrew Carnegie's U.S. Steel and Sergey Brin's Google, Inc.—all this was possible because of immigrants.

And then there are the countless names and the quiet acts that never made the history books but were no less consequential in building this country— the generations who braved hardship and great risk to reach our shores in search of a better life for themselves and their families; the millions of people, ancestors to most of us, who believed that there was a place where they could be, at long last, free to work and worship and live their lives in peace.

So this steady stream of hardworking and talented people has made America the engine of the global economy and a beacon of hope around the world. And it's allowed us to adapt and thrive in the face of technological and societal change. To this day, America reaps incredible economic rewards because we remain a magnet for the best and brightest from across the globe. Folks travel here in the hopes of being a part of a culture of entrepreneurship and ingenuity, and by doing so they strengthen and enrich that culture. Immigration also means we have a younger workforce—and a faster-growing economy—than many of our competitors. And in an increasingly interconnected world, the diversity of our country is a powerful advantage in global competition.

Just a few weeks ago, we had an event of small business owners at the White House. And one business owner was a woman named Prachee Devadas who came to this country, became a citizen, and opened up a successful technology services company. When she started, she had just one employee. Today, she employs more than a hundred people. This past April, we held a naturalization ceremony at the White House for members of our armed forces. Even though they were not yet citizens, they had enlisted. One of them was a woman named Perla Ramos—born and raised in Mexico, came to the United States shortly after 9/11, and she eventually joined the Navy. And she said, "I take pride in our flag and the history that forged this great nation and the history we write day by day."

These women, and men and women across this country like them, remind us that immigrants have always helped to build and defend this country—and that being an American is not a matter of blood or birth. It's a matter of faith. It's a matter of fidelity to the shared values that we all hold so dear. That's what makes us unique. That's what makes us strong. Anybody can help us write the next great chapter in our history.

Now, we can't forget that this process of immigration and eventual inclusion has often been painful. Each new wave of immigrants has generated fear and resentments towards newcomers, particularly in times of economic upheaval. Our founding was rooted in the notion that America was unique as a place of refuge and freedom for, in Thomas Jefferson's words, "oppressed humanity." But the ink on our Constitution was barely dry when, amidst conflict, Congress passed the Alien and Sedition Acts, which placed harsh restrictions of those suspected of having foreign allegiances. A century ago, immigrants from Ireland, Italy, Poland, other European countries were routinely subjected to rank discrimination and ugly stereotypes. Chinese immigrants were held in detention and deported from Angel Island in the San Francisco Bay. They didn't even get to come in.

So the politics of who is and who is not allowed to enter this country, and on what terms, has always been contentious. And that remains true today. And it's made worse by a failure of those of us in Washington to fix a broken immigration system.

To begin with, our borders have been porous for decades. Obviously, the problem is greatest along our Southern border, but it's not restricted to that part of the country. In fact, because we don't do a very good job of tracking who comes in and out of the country as visitors, large numbers avoid immigration laws simply by overstaying their visas.

The result is an estimated 11 million undocumented immigrants in the United States. The overwhelming majority of these men and women are simply seeking a better life for themselves and their children. Many settle in low-wage sectors of the economy; they work hard, they save, they stay out of trouble. But because they live in the shadows, they're vulnerable to unscrupulous businesses who pay them less than the minimum wage or violate worker safety rules—thereby putting companies who follow those rules, and Americans who rightly demand the minimum wage or overtime, at an unfair [dis]advantage. Crimes go unreported as victims and witnesses fear coming forward. And this makes it harder for the police to catch violent criminals and keep neighborhoods safe. And billions in tax revenue are lost each year because many undocumented workers are paid under the table.

More fundamentally, the presence of so many illegal immigrants makes a mockery of all those who are going through the process of immigrating legally. Indeed, after years of patchwork fixes and ill-conceived revisions, the legal immigration system is as broken as the borders. Backlogs and bureaucracy means the process can take years. While an applicant waits for approval, he or she is often forbidden from visiting the United States—which means even husbands and wives may be forced to spend many years apart. High fees and the need for lawyers may exclude worthy applicants. And while we provide students from around the world visas to get engineering and computer science degrees at our top universities, our laws discourage them from using those skills to start a business or power a new industry right here in the United States. Instead of training entrepreneurs to create jobs on our shores, we train our competition.

In sum, the system is broken. And everybody knows it. Unfortunately, reform has been held hostage to political posturing and special-interest wrangling—and to the pervasive sentiment in Washington that tackling such a thorny and emotional issue is inherently bad politics.

Just a few years ago, when I was a senator, we forged a bipartisan coalition in favor of comprehensive reform. Under the leadership of Senator Kennedy, who had been a longtime champion of immigration reform, and Senator John McCain, we worked across the aisle to help pass a bipartisan bill through the Senate. But that effort eventually came apart. And now, under the pressures of partisanship and election-year politics, many of the 11 Republican senators who voted for reform in the past have now backed away from their previous support.

Into this breach, states like Arizona have decided to take matters into their own hands. Given the levels of frustration across the country, this is understandable. But it is also ill conceived. And it's not just that the law Arizona passed is divisive—although it has fanned the flames of an already contentious debate. Laws like Arizona's put huge pressures on local law enforcement to enforce rules that ultimately are unenforceable. It puts pressure on already hard-strapped state and local budgets. It makes it difficult for people here illegally to report crimes—driving a wedge between communities and law enforcement, making our streets more dangerous and the jobs of our police officers more difficult.

And you don't have to take my word for this. You can speak to the police chiefs and others from law enforcement here today who will tell you the same thing.

These laws also have the potential of violating the rights of innocent American citizens and legal residents, making them subject to possible stops or questioning because of what they look like or how they sound. And as other states and localities go their own ways, we face the prospect that different rules for immigration will apply in different parts of the country—a patchwork of local immigration rules where we all know one clear national standard is needed.

Our task then is to make our national laws actually work—to shape a system that reflects our values as a nation of laws and a nation of immigrants. And that means being honest about the problem, and getting past the false debates that divide the country rather than bring it together.

For example, there are those in the immigrants' rights community who have argued passionately that we should simply provide those who are [here] illegally with legal status, or at least ignore the laws on the books and put an end to deportation until we have better laws. And often this argument is framed in moral terms: Why should we punish people who are just trying to earn a living?

I recognize the sense of compassion that drives this argument, but I believe such an indiscriminate approach would be both unwise and unfair. It would suggest to those thinking about coming here illegally that there will be no repercussions for such a decision. And this could lead to a surge in more illegal immigration. And it would also ignore the millions of people around the world who are waiting in line to come here legally.

Ultimately, our nation, like all nations, has the right and obligation to control its borders and set laws for residency and citizenship. And no matter how decent they are, no matter their reasons, the 11 million who broke these laws should be held accountable.

Now, if the majority of Americans are skeptical of a blanket amnesty, they are also skeptical that it is possible to round up and deport 11 million people. They know it's not possible. Such an effort would be logistically impossible and wildly expensive. Moreover, it would tear at the very fabric of this nation— because immigrants who are here illegally are now intricately woven into that fabric. Many have children who are American citizens. Some are children themselves, brought here by their parents at a very young age, growing up as American kids, only to discover their illegal status when they apply for college or a job. Migrant workers—mostly here illegally—have been the labor force of our farmers and agricultural producers for generations. So even if it was possible, a program of mass deportations would disrupt our economy and communities in ways that most Americans would find intolerable.

Now, once we get past the two poles of this debate, it becomes possible to shape a practical, common-sense approach that reflects our heritage and our values. Such an approach demands accountability from everybody—from government, from businesses and from individuals.

Government has a threshold responsibility to secure our borders. That's why I directed my Secretary of Homeland Security, Janet Napolitano—a former border governor—to improve our enforcement policy without having to wait for a new law.

Today, we have more boots on the ground near the Southwest border than at any time in our history. Let me repeat that: We have more boots on the ground on the Southwest border than at any time in our history. We doubled the personnel assigned to Border Enforcement Security Task Forces. We tripled the number of intelligence analysts along the border. For the first time, we've begun screening 100 percent of southbound rail shipments. And as a result, we're seizing more illegal guns, cash and drugs than in years past. Contrary to some of the reports that you see, crime along the border is down. And statistics collected by Customs and Border Protection reflect a significant reduction in the number of people trying to cross the border illegally.

So the bottom line is this: The southern border is more secure today than at any time in the past 20 years. That doesn't mean we don't have more work to do. We have to do that work, but it's important that we acknowledge the facts. Even as we are committed to doing what's necessary to secure our borders, even without passage of the new law, there are those who argue that we should not move forward with any other elements of reform until we have fully sealed our borders. But our borders are just too vast for us to be able to solve the problem only with fences and border patrols. It won't work. Our borders will not be secure as long as our limited resources are devoted to not only stopping gangs and potential terrorists, but also the hundreds of thousands who attempt to cross each year simply to find work.

That's why businesses must be held accountable if they break the law by deliberately hiring and exploiting undocumented workers. We've already begun to step up enforcement against the worst workplace offenders. And we're implementing and improving a system to give employers a reliable way to verify that their employees are here legally. But we need to do more. We cannot continue just to look the other way as a significant portion of our economy operates outside the law. It breeds abuse and bad practices. It punishes employers who act responsibly and undercuts American workers. And ultimately, if the demand for undocumented workers falls, the incentive for people to come here illegally will decline as well.

Finally, we have to demand responsibility from people living here illegally. They must be required to admit that they broke the law. They should be required to register, pay their taxes, pay a fine, and learn English. They must get right with the law before they can get in line and earn their citizenship—not just because it is fair, not just because it will make clear to those who might wish to come to America they must do so inside the bounds of the law, but because this is how we demonstrate that being—what being an American means. Being a citizen of this country comes not only with rights but also with certain fundamental responsibilities. We can create a pathway for legal status that is fair, reflective of our values, and works.

Now, stopping illegal immigration must go hand in hand with reforming our creaky system of legal immigration. We've begun to do that, by eliminating a backlog in background checks that at one point stretched back almost a year. That's just for the background check. People can now track the status of their immigration applications by email or text message. We've improved accountability and safety in the detention system. And we've stemmed the increases in naturalization fees. But here, too, we need to do more. We should make it easier for the best and the brightest to come to start businesses and develop products and create jobs.

Our laws should respect families following the rules—instead of splitting them apart. We need to provide farms a legal way to hire the workers they rely on, and a path for those workers to earn legal status. And we should stop punishing innocent young people for the actions of their parents by denying them the chance to stay here and earn an education and contribute their talents to build the country where they've grown up. The DREAM Act would do this, and that's why I supported this bill as a state legislator and as a U.S. senator—and why I continue to support it as president.

So these are the essential elements of comprehensive immigration reform. The question now is whether we will have the courage and the political will to pass a bill through Congress, to finally get it done. Last summer, I held a meeting with leaders of both parties, including many of the Republicans who had supported reform in the past—and some who hadn't. I was pleased to see a bipartisan framework proposed in the Senate by Senators Lindsey Graham and Chuck Schumer, with whom I met to discuss this issue. I've spoken with the Congressional Hispanic Caucus to plot the way forward and meet—and then I met with them earlier this week.

And I've spoken with representatives from a growing coalition of labor unions and business groups, immigrant advocates and community organizations, law enforcement, local government—all who recognize the importance of immigration reform. And I've met with leaders from America's religious communities, like Pastor Hybels—people of different faiths and beliefs, some liberal, some conservative, who nonetheless share a sense of urgency; who understand that fixing our broken immigration system is not only a political issue, not just an economic issue, but a moral imperative as well.

So we've made progress. I'm ready to move forward; the majority of Democrats are ready to move forward; and I believe the majority of Americans are ready to move forward. But the fact is, without bipartisan support, as we had just a few years ago, we cannot solve this problem. Reform that brings accountability to our immigration system cannot pass without Republican votes. That is the political and mathematical reality. The only way to reduce the risk that this effort will again falter because of politics is if members of both parties are willing to take responsibility for solving this problem once and for all.

And, yes, this is an emotional question, and one that lends itself to demagoguery. Time and again, this issue has been used to divide and inflame—and to demonize people. And so the understandable, the natural impulse among those who run for office is to turn away and defer this question for another day, or another year, or another administration. Despite the courageous leadership in the past shown by many Democrats and some Republicans—including, by the way, my predecessor, President Bush—this has been the custom. That is why a broken and dangerous system that offends our most basic American values is still in place.

But I believe we can put politics aside and finally have an immigration system that's accountable. I believe we can appeal not to people's fears but to their hopes, to their highest ideals, because that's who we are as Americans. It's been inscribed on our nation's seal since we declared our independence. "E pluribus unum." Out of many, one. That is what has drawn the persecuted and impoverished to our shores. That's what led the innovators and risk-takers from around the world to take a chance here in the land of opportunity. That's what has led people to endure untold hardships to reach this place called America.

One of the largest waves of immigration in our history took place little more than a century ago. At the time, Jewish people were being driven out of Eastern Europe, often escaping to the sounds of gunfire and the light from their villages burning to the ground. The journey could take months, as families crossed rivers in the dead of night, traveled miles by foot, endured a rough and dangerous passage over the North Atlantic. Once here, many made their homes in a teeming and bustling Lower Manhattan.

It was at this time that a young woman named Emma Lazarus, whose own family fled persecution from Europe generations earlier, took up the cause of these new immigrants. Although she was a poet, she spent much of her time advocating for better health care and housing for the newcomers. And inspired by what she saw and heard, she wrote down her thoughts and donated a piece of work to help pay for the construction of a new statue—the Statue of Liberty—which actually was funded in part by small donations from people across America.

Years before the statue was built—years before it would be seen by throngs of immigrants craning their necks skyward at the end of long and brutal voyage, years before it would come to symbolize everything that we cherish—she imagined what it could mean. She imagined the sight of a giant statue at the entry point of a great nation—but unlike the great monuments of the past, this would not signal an empire. Instead, it would signal one's arrival to a place of opportunity and refuge and freedom.

"Here at our sea-washed, sunset gates shall stand," she wrote,

A mighty woman with a torch…
From her beacon-hand
Glows world-wide welcome…
"Keep, ancient lands, your storied pomp!"…
"Give me your tired, and your poor,
Your huddled masses yearning to be free…
Send these, the homeless, tempest-tossed to me,
I lift my lamp beside the golden door!"

Let us remember these words. For it falls on each generation to ensure that that lamp—that beacon—continues to shine as a source of hope around the world, and a source of our prosperity here at home.

Thank you. God bless you. And may God bless the United States of America. Thank you.

According to Obama, how can we have an immigration system that is accountable or can be held accountable? Be specific in your answer.

In small groups, discuss how, according to President Obama, the U.S. immigration system is "broken." Describe how the U.S. immigration system is a political, an economic, and a moral issue.

Write a list of ideas on how the U.S. immigration system could be reformed. If you feel that the U.S. immigration system should not be reformed, list your reasons. Compare your list with the rest of the class.

Monsignor Arturo Bañuelas has been pastor of St. Pius X parish in El Paso, TX since 1988. Bañuelas is cofounder of the Academy of Catholic Hispanic Theologians in the U.S. He received a doctorate degree in Theology from the Gregorian University in Rome and is a strong leader in the El Paso, TX-Juárez, México border community, where he serves on numerous boards dealing with human rights and legal assistance for migrants. In this speech, Bañuelas spoke to over 700 residents of Juárez and El Paso who were protesting the drug war and asking for U.S. immigrants to be given equal rights. The rally took place on January 29, 2011 at the border fence at the end of Anapra Road, El Paso, TX.

PEACE AND JUSTICE WITHOUT BORDERS

By Msgr. Arturo Bañuelas

Rally 29 January 2011, Anapra Fence, El Paso, Texas

We are here today because we believe in justice and in the power of our united convictions to make a difference in our border area. We want a new Juárez and a new El Paso, cities that are the best places for our families to live in peace and harmony. Today, we demand no less than this.

We are here because we refuse to lay down in defeat before all the violence, killings, extortions, kidnappings, and beheadings that bloody our streets each day.

We are here because we are not afraid to stand up and speak up for what we believe. We will not be quiet any longer.

We are here to stand in solidarity with the victims of violence, with the families still crying for their lost loved ones, with the wounded, the scared, the disappeared, and the refugees.

An Immigration Reform Rally

We are here to denounce those in authority who pretend to protect us but instead lie, and participate in corruption, and in human rights violations.

We are here because we have a better non-violent solution to the problems that are destroying our lives along our border.

Right now we are living one of the worst crises in our border history. Juárez and El Paso are two lungs of the same body that was once a thriving cultural, social and economic community; but now both our community's futures are at stake. Hundreds of thousands of our hurting brothers and sisters are fleeing Juárez with trauma and unbearable desperation to a nation unwilling to legally welcome them. America this is not worthy of our country.

Over 3000 murders on our border is just too much blood running in our streets leaving unbearable scars of pain that will last a lifetime for fathers, mothers, brothers, sisters and friends. We are disgusted and feel angry about our women so savagely tortured and our friends so viciously executed and mutilated. Fear and violence have become a way of life that for some has no end in sight. Recently I had a funeral of a young man who was beheaded and his body was riddled with over 60 bullets. You can imagine the pain of his father who had to go identify the body of his dead son. At the funeral some of his friends pledged revenge for those who did this to their friend. I can understand their anger, but this is not the solution.

We know the causes of violence on our border: poverty, hunger, the growing gap between rich and poor, NAFTA policies that ignore the plight of the poor, racism, unjust immigration laws, bailing out wall street but not the poor who are losing their homes, illegal trafficking of guns going south, our U.S. lethal addiction for drugs that fund the cartel's terrorism of our border community, the militarization of our border which has already shown its deathly face, and the profiteering of selling violence to children in the media. The list is long and dreadful. These failed policies and laws serve only to bring dark results: people die; violence flows in our streets. But we can say very clearly today, no law, policy, or profit of violence has ever succeeded. Also it is time to say it clearly: when we buy and use drugs, even recreationally, we are paying for bullets that kill others, and we bring unbearable suffering to families.

We have a solution. Today we bring an alternative to all of this violence and death in our midst. It comes from our solidarity for peace. There is nothing stronger in this world than our united convictions in solidarity for peace. There is always a greater power at work in our solidarity for peace even in the midst of the forces of darkness that surround us. God put in every human heart this desire for peace.

However, the most significant reason for violence comes from our disconnection with each other. This distance translates into bloodshed, hate, carnage, and brutal hostility. Peace is born from our efforts to connect with each other and to value each other as sacred. We are all linked as one human family. We stand together or we fall together. We are each other, and we need to help each other. If I diminish you, I diminish myself. If I promote the good in you, I promote the goodness in me and also in everyone else at the same time. The road to peace is in our walking hand in hand with each other as one.

When we connect with one another, we live from our better side, and in us grows a profound desire to do good not bad. We desire more life, not death. We want to walk in our beauty, not our blood.

Our creator, God, made us good—not criminals, narcos, terrorists or murderers. This is why I still believe that there are more good people in the world than bad, and there is really more good in the world than bad, that we have an unbelievable capacity for goodness. And today we are here to celebrate the coming victory of our oneness over the violence of our divisions.

As long as there is violence toward each other, we all remain incomplete as human beings. At this time of such chaos and violence, when human life seems so dirt cheap, we much proclaim that each person matters, that they matter enormously to us, for we are each other. When we do this we are renewed as a people, the world turns toward peace as a better solution, and peace reigns. Violence is not the way to solve violence. We can break this vicious cycle of violence with our solidarity for peace.

I have been with many families who have lost loved ones to the violence in Juárez. Yet in my heart I feel hopeful for a new Juárez and a new El Paso because I can see in you a desire to live in solidarity for peace. I see before me a giant that is waking up and ready to roar. Today we can believe that in the end of all our human struggles, we will see that it is our oneness that will prevail over all violence. Victory comes in our togetherness. United for peace we win, not the narcos.

So today we have something important to say, and we want to say it loudly. It may look like Juárez is dying, that the narcos are taking over, and that there is no end in sight. But we are here in solidarity. We believe that we will rise again.

- Today we can feel confident that violence will not win in our El Paso-Juárez border as long as we stand together because we believe that we will rise again. If you believe it with me, say it out loud what you believe today: we believe that we will rise again.

- You may fill our streets with blood, our bodies with bullets, our souls with fear, but you will never take away our hope because we believe that we will rise again.

- It may look like the dark forces of violence have the upper hand, that we are out gunned, ill equipped and unprepared. But we are not backing down, and we will not be silent anymore because we believe that we will rise again.

- You can stomp on our work and try to break our lives with your murders, corruption, and terror, but we feel confident that your days are numbered because we have on our side a superior force that comes from our passion for peace. That's why we believe that we will rise again.

- We may feel wounded; our spirits may be down, our hearts disillusioned, our lives threatened, shaken in our beliefs in our capacity to overcome fear, but we are ready for the struggle and the victory because we believe that we will rise again.

- We are not afraid of the narcos, the threats, and the AK-47's, because from the sufferings of our brothers and sisters in Juárez and El Paso will emerge a stronger, more courageous border people because we believe that we will rise again.

Today is about our hope, not our fears. We are ready, and we will not give up in our quest for peace. In our solidarity peace is coming. And we tell the narcos: the future does not belong to you. It belongs to the fearless, courageous peacemakers who live in solidarity for peace. The future belongs to us, and we are ready to anticipate its joy, excitement, and peace.

This is an historic moment for us on the border. Let us commit ourselves to one another today. Embrace each other and see our future exploding in our midst. Do not live in fear. Be ready to show your resolve. Justice will triumph over hate, love will conquer violence, and our compassion will overcome our divisions.

Today we reach out to all the youth. Join us, not the narcos. Let us build together a new Juárez and El Paso. It is not too late.

I still believe in the dream of a better Juárez and El Paso. That is why we will not surrender to your bullets of fear. Hope runs through our veins and the cause of peace endures in our hearts. Justice is coming. Peace is at hand. We can feel confident today because God is on the side of peace. Let us become more passionately determined in our convictions for solidarity and its victory in our lives.

Ya Basta! Too many people have worked too hard, sacrificed too much; too much blood has been spilled for us to be bystanders in the emerging new border. Together we will prevail in the face of death. Amigos, amigas, we will rise again!

Msgr. Arturo J. Bañuelas, STD

29 enero 2011

Bañuelas shows a sense of urgency in his speech. What issues facing the border, the cities of El Paso and Juárez, drive Bañuelas to make this call to action? What specific action(s) is he asking for?

In his remarks on comprehensive immigration reform (page 33), President Obama states that fixing the U.S. immigration system is a "moral imperative." Would Bañuelas agree with the president's comment? Why or why not? What makes you think this way?

According to Bañuelas, the people on the El Paso-Juárez border are like "a giant that is waking up and is ready to roar." Later, he repeats, "We will rise again." In small groups, discuss how people living on, facing, or crossing borders in their lives can rise and let their voices be heard. What effects might such actions have?

Kevin Crust is a staff writer for the Los Angeles Times. *In this movie review, Crust critiques* A Day without a Mexican, *a movie portraying the experience of not having immigrants, for a day, in our country. Sergio Arau directed the movie.*

'A DAY WITHOUT A MEXICAN' IS PURE VANILLA

By Kevin Crust

Satire plays it safe despite its politically charged subject matter and fails to raise the important questions.

Arriving with a surprising amount of notoriety due to controversy from a billboard promotion, *A Day Without a Mexican* is a satire that is more bemusing than wicked. A film content to let some mild comedy carry its straightforward message rather than trying to say something more profound, it uses the well-trodden mockumentary form and a clever premise to drive home its point that Latinos are culturally, socially and economically underappreciated in California.

Directed by Sergio Arau (son of *Like Water for Chocolate* filmmaker Alfonso Arau), the movie opens with a white woman named Mary Jo Quintana (Maureen Flannigan) waking up to discover that her Latino husband, Roberto (Eduardo Palomo), has vanished along with their young son.

She soon learns that they are among the 14 million Latinos from across the state who have disappeared seemingly overnight.

This triggers the expected media frenzy, with pundits and scientists venturing guesses as to what is happening. A mysterious fog has shrouded the borders and coasts of California, blocking travel and communication with the outside world. Abandoned cars clog surface streets (but oddly enough, not freeways).

The ramifications for non-Latinos are immediate. With one-third of the workforce gone, the economy is a shambles. Among the missing are doctors and lawyers, police officers and firefighters, gardeners and cooks.

There are no migrant workers to harvest the abundant fields of the San Joaquin Valley, effectively cutting off the supply of fresh produce. Schools are closed because, as a graphic helpfully points out, 20% of the state's kindergarten through 12th grade teachers are Latino.

The film's protagonist is Lila Rod (Yareli Arizmendi, the director's wife and co-writer of the screenplay), a Latina newscaster urged by her station manager to reinstate the —riguez to her surname and roll her Rs to maximize her Latino-ness. Lila inexplicably doesn't disappear, and she becomes a media target herself.

For a film taking on such blatantly political subject matter, *A Day Without a Mexican* is oddly inoffensive. The portrayal of a Pete Wilson-like state senator (John Getz) who made his name as an anti-immigration proponent and ascends to acting governor during the crisis is balanced by an enlightened grower (Muse Watson), who pines for his best friend, Jose (Joaquin Garrido).

Arau and Arizmendi, with help from co-writer Sergio Guerrero, expanded to feature-length their 1998 short, also called "A Day Without a Mexican." Unfortunately, the movie feels like exactly that, a fine concept for a short stretched beyond its capacity. Much of the humor is overly familiar, and the broader elements feel strained when it veers toward melodrama in its final third.

Plotwise, the movie doesn't make a lot of sense. The extended running time gives you time to question things such as why doesn't this mysterious fog cause even more calamity? After all, with communication completely cut off, wouldn't institutions like banks have some difficulty? Shouldn't there be rioting? What about the large power grids we learned so much about during the rolling blackouts of a few years ago? Why are the local television stations able to broadcast?

None of these questions are ultimately very important, but they are the type that arise when the mind isn't given enough to do during a movie. Even the overarching question of what happened to the Latinos goes essentially unanswered, even once the crisis is resolved, making for a pretty limp ending.

The movie is at its most successful when it parodies the news coverage of the events. Glib newscasters and politicians mangling cultural nuances is always good for a laugh. The film's title alludes to the disparaging way that Latinos, regardless of where they are from, are frequently labeled as "Mexicans."

The filmmakers are rather generous in their assessment of mankind. The movie doesn't simply write off the contemporary Latino's plight to the evils of bias and hatred. It sees it as a residue of ignorance and aims to educate.

As satire, however, the film is toothless. It doesn't ask the important questions of why the situation continues. It's satisfied to point out an injustice without going any deeper, satisfied to remain infotainment, distributing some facts amid the laughs that may make a few people ponder but won't necessarily ruffle any feathers.

Perhaps it is the filmmakers' intent to make that one bold statement—"Notice us! Appreciate us!"—and then move on. There is something to be said about keeping a politically charged message simple, but it also feels safe and geared to maximize the box office.

Using the internet or resources available through your library, explain what satire is. Based on your research, what makes a satirical text effective? How can satire go wrong or fail? Does Crust see the movie as being successful or unsuccessful satire? What kinds of evidence does he provide to support his position?

After watching the movie *A Day without a Mexican*, write a review of it. Be sure to set criteria for your evaluation of the movie. Provide specific examples from the movie to support your evaluation.

In this chapter from his book, The Other Face of America, *Jorge Ramos explores what the U.S. would be like in a day without Mexican immigrants. He uses the movie,* A Day Without a Mexican *as a starting point for this chapter.*

A DAY WITHOUT A MEXICAN

By Jorge Ramos
Translated by Patricia J. Duncan

What would happen if all of a sudden all the Mexicans who lived in the United States disappeared? Yes, all of them, the more than 7 million Mexicans who were born in México but live here in the United States.

A similar question crossed the mind of film director Sergio Arau, and through what he called a "false documentary," he tried to answer it. I saw several scenes from the movie and what stood out, with both humor and insight, was the enormous importance of the Latino population in the United States. Giving an original twist to one of the most overused sayings—"You never know what you have until you lose it"—Arau has managed to capture on film what many have thought and hinted at for years: If all the Mexicans disappeared for a day, the U.S. economy would be seriously hindered.

The movie focuses on what would happen if all the Mexicans in the state of California, where most Mexicans in the United States live, suddenly and inexplicably disappeared. Let's try and imagine this.

A day without a Mexican in California would mean losses in the millions in the orange, avocado, lettuce, and grape industries. Supermarkets would be without fruit and vegetables, and wine shops without those famous California whites and reds. (According to the 1990 census, slightly less than 15 percent of all Mexicans in the United States, legal and undocumented, work in agriculture.)

A day without a Mexican in California would mean a complete halt in the construction and garment industries, among many others. (Approximately 35 percent of Mexicans in the Untied States work in these sectors.)

A day without a Mexican in California would show that hotels, restaurants, stores, markets, gas stations, and offices depend on those workers who cross the southern border of the Untied States. (More than half of Mexicans in the United States are employed in the service industry.)

A day without a Mexican in California would mean that thousands of English-speaking men and women would not be able to go to work because their nannies would not show up to take care of their children and babies.

A day without a Mexican in California would leave the television and radio stations with the largest audiences in the Los Angeles areas—which transmit in Spanish, although few are aware of this—without viewers or listeners.

A day without a Mexican in California would give the false impression that the official language in the United States is English.

A day without a Mexican in California would mean cancelled operations because doctors would not arrive, unkept court appointments because lawyers would not show up, and unfulfilled commitments because of absent executives.

Contrary to the trite stereotype that all Mexicans in the United States are poorly educated and are gardeners and work in the fields, the 1990 census revealed that there were 3,869 immigrants, born in México, who held doctorate degrees. That tears the stereotype to shreds. It is worth mentioning that Mexican labor, in U.S. fields and gardens, just as in the assembly plants on the border, is considered among the best and most efficient in the world.

The exercise of magical migration where we make more than 7 million Mexicans disappear just like that can be applied to other Hispanic groups in the United States with the same results. For example, what would become of Miami without the Cubans and Nicaraguans? Or New York without the Puerto Ricans and Dominicans? Or New Orleans without the Hondurans? Or Los Angeles without the Salvadorans and Guatemalans? What would become of the U.S. Army without the 7.90 percent of its soldiers who call themselves "Latinos"? Unfortunately, the positive impact of the presence of the more than 30 million Hispanics in the United States is not always recognized and appreciated by the rest of the population, despite their enormous cultural, social, and economic contributions.

Nevertheless, there are people who do not want us here in the United States. I received a phone call from a young man who had heard about the subject of Arau's movie—*A Day Without a Mexican*—and he had the arrogance to tell me that, deep down, nothing would make him happier than if all Mexicans were to disappear from the map. Naturally, I hung up on him before he had finished speaking, so he would see for himself just what would happen if all Mexicans in the United States disappeared for a day. I wouldn't be surprised if the dreams of former California governor Pete Wilson and the xenophobic conservative Pat Buchanan were just like the wishes of that impertinent man who called me.

The United States has still not accepted its multiethnic and multicultural makeup. It has still not realized—or simply does not want to recognize—that the children in our families are not all white anymore. The "little brown ones," as former President George Bush said of his grandchildren of Hispanic origin—his son Jeb is married to a Mexican, Columba—are increasing in number.

It is a shame that Arau's short film was turned down by the organizers of the main film festivals in the United States. *A Day Without a Mexican* would reveal to the United States the country they are really living in, a country far from the black-and-white one they have instilled in their minds.

POSTSCRIPT: The ultraconservative politician Pat Buchanan would enjoy a day without a Mexican in the United States. In a 1995 television interview (which was quoted by the *New York Times*), the eternally unsuccessful presidential candidate, when asked what he would do should he get to the White House, said, "I will stop illegal immigration cold by putting a double-linked security fence along the two hundred miles of the border where millions pour in every year."

There are three errors, however, in that argument. First, if Buchanan wants to put up a double-linked fence along two hundred miles of border, what will he do along the other 1,800 miles? Second, Buchanan does not understand that undocumented immigration is a problem of supply and demand of jobs, not laws and fences. Buchanan's third error is that with such racist views, he will never be president of a multicultural country such as the United States.

That is a relief.

Explore

What proof of Latinos' cultural, social, and economic contributions does Ramos provide in his article? Is the proof credible? Convincing? Why or why not?

Invent

How, according to Ramos, can people show their acceptance and respect for multiethnic, multicultural, and/or multilingual diversity in U.S. society today? Give specific examples.

Compose

How would your life be different in a day without Mexicans, Latinos, or other immigrants? Or would it not affect you in any way? Write an essay in which you describe how having or not having immigrants in your life would change your life. Think of all the aspects of your life—personal, financial, educational, professional, moral, cultural, etc.—and be specific with your rationale and examples.

Jorge Ramos has been a lead anchor for Noticiero Univision, *a popular news show watched by millions of Spanish households in the U.S. for over 20 years. Ramos has received Emmy awards and has published numerous books. In addition, Ramos has a daily radio commentary and weekly newspaper column.*

HELIODORO'S LETTERS AND THE MEXICAN GIRL WHO WROTE TO PRESIDENT CLINTON

By Jorge Ramos
Translated by Patricia J. Duncan

Proposition 187 in California demonstrated that a large part of the U.S. population erroneously considered the undocumented immigrants to be responsible for the main problems in the United States. When Californians approved Proposition 187 on November 8, 1994, their vote approved one of the most radical and unfair anti-immigrant laws in recent memory. Despite having been approved by voters, Proposition 187 was overturned in the courts for being unconstitutional. Nevertheless, had it taken effect, it would have denied education and medical attention to hundreds of thousands of undocumented immigrants.

Then-governor Pete Wilson was quickly identified with Proposition 187. The proposition was based on the idea that immigrants were coming to California to take advantage of free education and medical services. Studies, however, indicated something much different.

According to a study carried by *U.S. News & World Report* (October 4, 1993), which included the analysis of 12.5 million documents from the Census Bureau: "Contrary to popular belief, immigrants do not rob citizens of jobs but either expand employment niches or take jobs few Americans want." Likewise, the magazine stated, "Most newcomers do not rely on welfare... overall only about four percent of new immigrants receive welfare aid."

This kind of reasoning had no impact. Only a judge was able to put an end to the most radical anti-immigration law in the history of California and, possibly, the history of the United States.

While all this was going on, I received copies of two letters that a Mexican, whom I will refer to only as Heliodoro, sent to the then-governor of California and to former Mexican president Carlo Salinas de Gortari. Both letters were written in 1993. He asked me to share them:

Mr. Governor Pete Wilson:

My greatest wish is that you read this letter that expresses what I feel. As a Mexican, I came to this country at the age of fifteen. I have now been working here for eighteen years and earning minimum wage. I began to work at the age of sixteen because I didn't want to be a burden to anyone. I have kept almost every pay stub from all these years. I have always tried not to be a burden to society. And many of my race, just like me, have done the same.

But sometimes you can't cope with so many bills, and hospitals that charge you without regard. With the little that we earn, we have no other choice but to ask for public assistance in order to survive and to not let our children or ourselves die. How I wish you and others like you were in our shoes.

It is not true that the women come to give birth here because of the great fortune that welfare gives them. I have two children. If what you say is true, I would have twelve children. I accept that among my race we have everything… just like the other races. No race is perfect. If you believe that the illegal Mexicans are to blame for the problems in this country, we should be living like kings and not like we are, working from sunup to sundown for a miserable wages, without paid vacations or holidays and, on top of that, being treated poorly by our bosses. We have no job security, and they pay us minimum wage… if we want it. And if not, they say "*alli esta la puerta abierta.*" And they say it just like that because most do not know English and even less a high school diploma, which is what is needed to get a better paying job.

Mr. Governor, if the illegals stopped coming, do you think the problems would end? I don't. Who would the bad leaders blame then?

Sincerely,
Heliodoro R.

Mr. Carlos Salinas de Gortari
President of the Republic of México

Mr. President:

I am writing this letter with the hope that you will read it. I have been living in California since 1975. I came with the hope of returning to México as soon as we had an honest and fair president in office, a president who would remove the bad leaders from cities and towns, a president who could establish order and rid the country of corruption.

I was compelled to write this letter because here in the United States we are insulted and humiliated. We, the Mexican immigrants, are looked down on. It is not right that we must suffer so many injustices at the hands of the employers who make us work without job security and pay us minimum wage. If they can, they pay us less than if they were doing us a favor giving us work. Aside from that, the American government is accusing us of coming to exploit this country. They want to make us look like sewer rats. We can't take it anymore.

With our work we are enriching this country, which is not ours thanks to México's former presidents. We, the poor, don't even have the freedom to choose them, even though we are the majority. Let the people decide which party and which religion they want, and let them have freedom of speech. Now, at the end of the twentieth century, do not impose leaders on us.

We need someone who will lead us with honesty and fairness, someone who will help us save the country with our effort and our will. Our México will no longer be a mediocre country that does not know when it can repay the debts that every president has been increasing. That is why we want a president who loves the people and his race as he loves himself.

Think about it. It's difficult, but not impossible.

> Sincerely, A fellow countryman.
> Heliodoro R.

POSTSCRIPT: In his letters, Heliodoro hit the nail on the head. There are two main causes for immigration from México to the United States—one that pushes the Mexican to the north and the other that draws him to the United States. But as the Mexican crosses the border, the problems are just beginning.

Far from being the earthly paradise that was imagined, the United States turns into a kind of labyrinth, an obstacle course. Heliodoro's letters reflect the resentment and frustration of an immigrant, as much with the homeland he left behind as with the circumstances he must face after his arrival in the north.

THE MEXICAN GIRL WHO WROTE TO PRESIDENT CLINTON

© Jim Epler Photography

A view of a little girl eating lunch on the U.S.-México Border.

In 1997, I received a letter that a Mexican girl had written to the then-president of the United States, Bill Clinton. She did not want her name to be revealed, but she did want Clinton and Americans to know how the immigration laws were negatively affecting the future of many immigrant families like hers in the United States. She had been living with her family in Texas for six years, until the climate of persecution, and the impossibility of resolving their legal status, forced them to return to the Mexican state of Puebla.

This is the letter from a little girl who had the courage to tell the president what many others just like her were experiencing. The letter said:

Dear President Clinton:

I do not know if anyone will ever read this letter, but I hope that someone does. Whenever someone reads this letter, hopefully it will be Mr. Clinton, by then I will be back in my native country, México.

I was born in Puebla, in México, in the year 1981. I will be sixteen years old in June, and in June it will have been six years that I am here in the United States. I am a straight-A student and have been ever since I began school. I have earned the respect of my peers and of other people whom I love, and they love me, too. I have received many academic awards as well as athletic awards. I have even won a Presidential Award. I have been involved in many basketball, volleyball, soccer, softball, and track teams. I keep my grades up and at the same time I'm involved in other programs, such as student council. I am also the president of D-FYIT, a program to keep kids off of drugs, and you name it. I've been enrolled in many other programs.

When I got to the United States, I looked at the United States as the place where one could make their dreams come true. The "place" of liberty and freedom. When my family and I migrated into the United States, it was only my mom, my dad, my brother, and me. Now I have a three-year-old brother who was born here and is an American citizen and has all the privilages *[sic]* and rights any American citizen has. We were finally beginning to get stable in one place, and finally living a "nice life," but because of all the new laws that have been approved and the ones that are to come, we have to return to our country, México. As you can now tell, we don't "belong here." My parents, one of my brothers, and me, are illegal aliens that came to the United States in search of a better life, and to find freedom. I was ten years old when we came to the United States, and I guess that one could say that a ten-year-old cannot distinguish right from wrong.

But now, I am a mature sixteen-year-old who can distinguish right from wrong, now I can say that I was "wrong" to believe in what I did as a child. A child that dreamed too much and a child that knew "nothing" about "anything."

One cannot blame anyone for certain situations, but because laws have been passed and approved, I have to leave behind good friends that I made, and I have to forget those goals and dreams that I had for my future. It is going to be very hard for all my family, but because my family is strong mentally, physically, and spiritually, we believe that we will survive this adversity. Now we have to go back and start "living" once again. All I want you to know is that we never came in search of your money. All my family and I wanted was a chance to become individuals that were worthy citizens.

Thank you for your time.
M.G.

POSTSCRIPT: I sent a copy of this letter to the White House. But I do not know if President Clinton ever read it.

Explore

Research California's Proposition 187. What did it propose? What is its status now? What are Heliodoro's frustrations as an immigrant in the United States and as a citizen of his homeland, México?

Collaborate

In small groups, discuss both Heliodoro's letters and the Mexican girl's letter. Which letter is more persuasive? Why?

Compose

Write a letter, as a college student, to the president of your homeland. Provide a rationale, either supporting or opposing immigrants' place in your country. Be persuasive. Use ethos, logos, and pathos when giving reasons for your argument.

Sandra Cisneros is an author and poet whose books include The House on Mango Street, Caramelo, Vintage Cisneros, *and a children's book,* Hairs/Pelitos. The House on Mango Street *won the Before Columbus Foundation's American Book Award in 1985 and is required reading in middle schools, high schools, and universities across the U.S. Cisneros has been a recipient of many awards and honors, including, in 1995, the MacArthur Foundation Fellowship. She has been a college recruiter, teacher, counselor to high school dropouts, and a visiting writer at numerous universities. She currently resides in San Antonio, TX.*

NO SPEAK ENGLISH

By Sandra Cisneros

Mamacita is the big mama of the man across the street, third-floor front. Rachel says her name ought to be *Mamasota*, but I think that's mean.

The man saved his money to bring her here. He saved and saved because she was alone with the baby boy in that country. He worked two jobs. He came home late and he left early. Every day.

Then one day *Mamacita* and the baby boy arrived in a yellow taxi. The taxi door opened like a waiter's arm. Out stepped a tiny pink shoe, a foot soft as a rabbit's ear, then the thick ankle, a flutter of hips, fuchsia roses and green perfume. The man had to pull her; the taxicab driver had to push. Push, pull. Push, pull. Poof!

All at once she bloomed. Huge, enormous, beautiful to look at, from the salmon-pink feather on the tip of her hat down to the little rosebuds of her toes. I couldn't take my eyes off her tiny shoes.

Up, up, up the stairs she went with the baby boy in a blue blanket, the man carrying her suitcases, her lavender hatboxes, a dozen boxes of satin high heels. Then we didn't see her. Somebody said because she's too fat, somebody because of the three flights of stairs, but I believe she doesn't come out because she is afraid to speak English, and maybe this is so since she only knows eight words. She knows to say: *He not here* for when the landlord comes, *No speak English* if anybody else comes, and *Holy smokes*. I don't know where she learned this, but I heard her say it one time and it surprised me.

My father says when he came to this country he ate hamandeggs for three months. Breakfast, lunch and dinner. Hamandeggs. That was the only word he knew. He doesn't eat hamandeggs anymore.

Whatever her reasons, whether she is fat, or can't climb the stairs, or is afraid of English, she won't come down. She sits all day by the window and plays the Spanish radio show and sings all the homesick songs about her country in a voice that sounds like a seagull.

Home. Home. Home is a house in a photograph, a pink house, pink as hollyhocks with lots of startled light. The man paints the walls of the apartment pink, but it's not the same, you know. She still sighs for her pink house, and then I think she cries. I would.

Sometimes the man gets disgusted. He starts screaming and you can hear it all the way down the street.

Ay, she says, she is sad.

Oh, he says. Not again.

Cuándo, cuándo, cuándo? she asks.

Ay, caray! We *are* home. This *is* home. Here I am and here I stay. Speak English. Speak English. Christ!

Ay! Mamacita, who does not belong, every once in a while lets out a cry, hysterical, high, as if he had torn the only skinny thread that kept her alive, the only road out to that country.

And then to break her heart forever, the baby boy, who has begun to talk, starts to sing the Pepsi commercial he heard on T.V.

No speak English, she says to the child who is singing in the language that sounds like tin. No speak English; no speak English, and bubbles into tears. No, no, no, as if she can't believe her ears.

What is Cisneros telling the reader about language? About English? About a person's home language? How do you know this? Do you see any "linguistic borders" in this vignette?   What are these?

Write an essay supporting a law requiring immigrants to learn English in the United States and/or supporting immigrants' right to their home language.

Isabel Baca received a PhD in Rhetoric and Professional Communication from New Mexico State University in Las Cruces, NM. She is an Assistant Professor of English at the University of Texas at El Paso, where she created and maintains the Community Writing Partners Program. A native El Pasoan, Baca teaches bilingual workplace writing courses and the Community Literacy Internship course. Baca focuses her outreach efforts and research on the El Paso, TX-Juárez, Mexico border community.

EXPLORING DIVERSITY, BORDERS, AND STUDENT IDENTITIES: A BILINGUAL SERVICE-LEARNING WORKPLACE WRITING APPROACH

BY ISABEL BACA

I am my language. Until I can take pride in my language, I cannot take pride in myself.

—Gloria Anzaldúa

Being situated on an international border allows higher-education institutions to explore diverse cultural and linguistic venues for teaching and learning. Such is the case for workplace writing courses at the University of Texas at El Paso. Workplace writing, intercultural communication, service-learning, and bilingualism became the tools for exploring diversity, strengthening student identities, and bridging disciplinary, geographical, cultural, and linguistic borders. This article includes the voices of service-learning students, agency mentors, and faculty involved in an English-Spanish workplace writing course and shows how service-learning empowers students to explore and strengthen their diverse identities.

Redesigning the National Alliance of Mental Illness newsletter. Serving as English-Spanish translators at the Las Americas Immigrant Advocacy Center. Revising and translating pamphlets for the Child Crisis Center. Researching and assisting in writing grants for Big Brothers Big Sisters of El Paso. Helping adult learners prepare résumés and job applications letters at La Mujer Obrera

Center. These are but a few examples of the tasks performed by bilingual service-learning workplace writing students at the University of Texas, El Paso (UTEP).

Workplace writing in the Department of English at UTEP is offered both monolingually and bilingually with service-learning as an option. Within the context of the workplace writing, intercultural communication, service-learning, and bilingualism became the primary tools for exploring diversity, strengthening student identities, and bridging borders: disciplinary (academic and workplace), geographical (United States and México), cultural (American, Mexican-American, and Mexican), and linguistic (English and Spanish).

THE CONTEXT FOR THE COURSE

UTEP is ideally positioned to create diverse cultural and linguistic venues for teaching and learning. El Paso, Texas/Juárez, México border residents are exposed to English and Spanish, daily and both languages play major roles in the extended community. More than 70% of El Paso households speak a language other than English as the primary language, and 97% of these families speak Spanish at home (Scenters-Zapico). Border residents are also exposed to numerous cultures, making El Paso a truly multicultural community. At UTEP, nearly 72% of the student body is Hispanic and another 10% are Mexican nationals (UTEP University Communications).

Many El Paso/Juárez residents commute daily from one country to the other. They may cross the international bridge to attend school, go to work, find entertainment, or visit family. Interaction between and dependence on each other are what make these two sister cities, El Paso and Juárez, function as a single bilingual, multicultural community.

With UTEP's distinctive student population and local community in mind, UTEP's Department of English is continually exploring community outreach venues, including service learning courses. Workplace writing is one such course, and we offer the class both monolingually (English only) and bilingually (in which students are required to produce documents and give presentations in both English and Spanish). In both versions of the course, students are given an option to serve as workplace writing/communication consultants for non-profit organizations such as Big Brothers Big Sisters of El Paso, Centro de Salud Familiar La Fe, and the El Paso Hispanic Chamber of Commerce. All students, whether or not they take the service learning option, are required to complete various written and oral assignments: memos, e-mail correspondence, bad news letters, proposals, project presentations, progress reports, peer critique reviews, résumés and job application letters, team performance evaluations, and final professional reports and oral presentations.

The workplace writing course, a required course for all business majors, has been taught at UTEP for many years. It was not taught bilingually, however, until 2000, when a grant first funded the *Bilingual Professional Writing Certificate* project. To be certified, English-Spanish bilingual students must complete each of the four required courses with a grade B or better and must receive a satisfactory score on a bilingual exit exam administered and evaluated by a committee comprised of faculty from the Departments of English and Languages and Linguistics. The required courses are: (1) a bilingual section of either *Workplace Writing* or *Technical Writing*; (2) a bilingual section of the *Senior Writing Practicum*; (3) *Introduction to Translation*; and (4) either *Commercial and Legal Translation*, *Translation from the Information Media*, or *Literary Translation*.

The first bilingual section of Workplace Writing was piloted in spring 2000, and because of its success, bilingual sections of this course have been taught every semester since. In addition to students pursuing the Bilingual Professional Writing Certificate, students who are confident in their English-Spanish bilingualism and want to practice both languages also enroll in the bilingual section. Given UTEP's student population, these sections are full to their capacity (25 students) and at times multiple bilingual sections are offered.

The objectives of the workplace writing course (taught in English only) center on having students learn how to make critical decisions in professional contexts. Principles of professional rhetoric and strategies for the different stages of the composing process in both written and oral communication for the workplace contexts are applied and emphasized. The bilingual section of the workplace writing course requires students to produce workplace documents and give oral presentations in both languages, using professional rhetoric principles and composing strategies as well.

PRINCIPLES GUIDING COURSE DESIGN

UTEP's bilingual workplace writing class was designed with several key principles in mind. Workplace writing instructors who teach classes comprised primarily of second-language learners face distinct challenges. Janet Bean and her colleagues ask, "Should We Invite Students to Write in Home Languages?" and conclude that the question is not whether writing instructors should invite students to write in their mother tongue, but rather, "when and under what conditions" (225-39). English-Spanish bilingual workplace writing courses provide ideal conditions. These courses allow second language students to utilize, practice, and improve their full range of linguistic resources and skills in both their languages. This type of course embraces diversity, both linguistically and culturally, and, very importantly, encourages students to recognize their bilingualism as an asset, not as an obstacle to writing and communicating in their second language.

The National Commission on Writing similarly urges educators who teach bilingual or dual language students to build on these learners' language strengths and concludes that students who learn to write in two languages simultaneously may learn more than those who only practice one language (34). By practicing both languages and seeing the critical need for both, students can come to appreciate the value of all languages and the importance of being able to communicate with diverse cultures in the workplace and the community.

The American Council on the Teaching of Foreign Languages (ACTFL) not only endorses these goals, but offers guidelines that support service-learning as a strong and effective pedagogical practice for achieving them, setting standards for what foreign language students should know and be able to do. These standards focus on *communication, communities, cultures, comparisons,* and *connections*. Students enrolled in the bilingual workplace writing course meet the ACTFL guidelines in multidimensional and inter-related ways. They use both Spanish and English, in written and oral forms, to *communicate* within a workplace setting and *cultural* context, holding face-to-face conversations, participating in class discussions and peer critique sessions, and giving oral presentations. Students *compare and contrast* the different dialects, values, and norms involved in professional contexts and intercultural communication, particularly as these apply on the United States/México border. Students also compare academic discourse to workplace discourse and discover how these are different and how they must be able to use both to succeed in academia and the workplace. Students explore how they belong to different cultures and use and practice different discourses; they begin to connect to others outside the classroom and experience a sense of community, becoming more aware of their community, its diversity, and its communication needs. By writing documents, such as memos, letters, reports, promotional items, and web pages, and by giving presentations and translating, students practice real business communication, learn about their community's needs, and realize the power language holds in society.

In addition to experiencing a sense of community and learning their community's literacy needs, students practice writing outside academia, making service-learning an effective teaching and learning methodology. As Stuart Stewart argues in "Crossing Borders/ Forging Identities" and Melody Bowdon and J. Blake Scott demonstrate in "Service-Learning in Technical and Professional Communication," community-based learning allows students to conduct significant projects that cause them to interact with community members and ultimately improve the community, school, and/or students' lives.

Kathryn Rentz and Ashley Mattingly, in "Selling Peace in a Time of War: The Rhetorical and Ethical Challenges of a Graduate-Level Service-Learning Course," argue that if a writing instructor's goal is to prepare students for writing careers, the focus of the service-learning course should be on writing and developing as strong professional ethic, not on "doing good." In other words, writing well and doing good work for the agencies and the community should be primary, and civic responsibility and caring for others should take a secondary role. I contend that service-learning workplace writing students have an equal opportunity to do both; they can grow as professional writers and still "do good" for the community. Students can learn while serving, and serve while learning. The challenge is in structuring the course carefully, placing students appropriately, and communicating effectively with the three key parties involved—the agency mentor, the student, and the writing instructor.

COURSE DESIGN

The service-learning component was first integrated in the bilingual workplace writing course in Spring 2005. Students who wish to earn extra credit and be exempt from one of the writing assignments can choose the service-learning option and are then required to serve as bilingual communicators for a non-profit organization for a minimum of twenty hours during the semester. A list of potential agencies is provided, but students have the freedom to work with an organization of their choice with the instructor's approval. Students complete agreement forms with their agency mentors and submit descriptions of the communication tasks they will complete in English and Spanish for the agencies. Students are required to keep evaluation forms. At midterm, students give oral progress reports on their service, and at the end of the semester, they give final presentations to the class, reflecting on their service as bilingual communicators. Thus, students must meet both course and agency requirements to receive full credit for the service-learning option.

Recruiting a diverse group of non-profit organizations provides the students with a better understanding of the communication and literacy needs of the community and helps in successfully matching students with appropriate agencies, based on the agencies' needs and students' different skills and identities. Following Paul Heilker's principles for ensuring that placements will be of benefit to the student, agency, and the community (72), non-profit agencies are asked to describe their needs, which vary in type, degree, and urgency. Agencies are also asked to complete an agency profile and name the person who will act as the agency mentor for service-learning students. The following is a list of some of the self-described communication and literacy needs of several non-profit organizations:

Women's Intercultural Center

"It would be beneficial to have someone who is bilingual. We can prepare a practicum for someone who is not, but we would prefer someone who is. The population we serve and the audience for our correspondence and marketing materials are both English speaking and Spanish speaking. We could also accommodate someone who can or needs to work from home as long as he or she has a computer and e-mail access."

Advocacy Center for the Children of El Paso

"We are very interested in developing/translating child abuse identification and awareness brochures and training materials in Spanish."

Las Americas Immigrant Advocacy Center

"Bilingual students are welcome, because we do translations for cases."

AVANCE

"We run an educational program: early childhood development, parenting, and adult literacy for low income families with young children. We are interested in a student newsletter or storybook."

Feedback from agency mentors also highlights the successes or glitches of the matching process. At the end of the semester, one agency mentor wrote: "It would have helped if *our* program were not in so much flux due to underfunding and general underdevelopment of this sector of the workforce which affects the efficiency of limited-time volunteer hours in general, but overall it was a very good match of skills to needs." This agency mentor continued, "I wasn't sure if someone so young could work well with mature adult learners who are learning English and Spanish written skills for office work, but she has done an excellent job….[This student] is going places! I hope she will continue with us in some other capacity, as she has the 'right stuff' for this Center." Such evaluations from agency mentors show the positive impact student volunteers have on the community and demonstrate how bilingual student communicators help meet important needs.

Guest speakers from different workplace settings who are bilingual and who understand the importance of effective intercultural communication are important contributors to the success of the course. Speaking to the students in both languages, these guests stress the importance of knowing two or more languages and understanding not only the language but the culture of an intended audience. For example, in fall 2006, Jesus Manuel Muñoz Delgado, Vice-President of Merchandising and Marketing of the S-Mart supermarkets in México (a 34-store chain with warehouses on both sides of the U.S.-México border), visited the bilingual workplace writing class and spoke to the students about how knowing the language is not enough when conducting business in other countries. Knowing the culture is also essential. Muñoz spends considerable time using both English and Spanish since he works with different suppliers and consultants from México, Argentina, and the United States. He stressed how even a single language changes from country to country and within the same country. Argentinian Spanish is not the same as Mexican Spanish, and the Spanish spoken on the U.S.-México border is not the same as the Spanish spoken in México City. Dialects come into play, and to be effective communicators, international entrepreneurs and business negotiators must know and understand the norms, values, and protocols of the cultures where they work. Muñoz commended the students for enrolling in a bilingual workplace communication course, confirming that, especially with the experience they gain working with community organizations, they will be at a tremendous advantage when they enter the job market.

WORKPLACE WRITING AND STUDENT IDENTITY

Service-learning students in the workplace writing course explore their identities in multiple ways. They explore different cultures and discover their membership in more than one—they belong to an academic culture, workplace culture, ethnic culture, gender culture, language culture, and more. Students explore their multiple identities through service-learning and learn that communicating with diverse cultures and serving others can make them stronger and more productive. One student, Flor, wrote the following reflection:

> I have been involved in doing many tasks for this organization. I started off by just doing anything that had to do with workplace writing. I translate documents from English to Spanish/Spanish to English. I also help them by creating spreadsheet templates for the organization and writing training modules for the students. I also provide help for students when writing their résumé and cover letter in Spanish, by translating it to English and making the necessary corrections. After working with La Mujer Obrera for about two weeks I got involved with working directly with students. I teach and reinforce English skills both oral and written. Aside from teaching Basic English, I tutor and provide the essential help needed to facilitate their Citizenship class. To me this is very important because as I tutor I reinforce my own historical knowledge…This experience has really changed me for good not only professionally but personally as well. I have grown in all aspects and I have built a strong relationship with my mentor as well as with my students…Volunteering at La Mujer Obrera has really opened my eyes towards reality and it has showed me the importance of getting involved with my community.

Azucena, a student who served as a bilingual communicator and writer at La Posada Home, a shelter for women and their children, concluded:

> This semester has given me the opportunity to seek a learning experience outside of the normal university settings…As students in the undergraduate level, we become absorbed with ourselves and our career goals. We forget that there is a whole other world waiting

for us to reach out…..Some of us never stop and reflect upon our real surroundings. We can make a difference now!

Through the service-learning, workplace writing course, traditionally marginalized populations are given the opportunity to learn to reach across boundaries and bridge cultural, linguistic, and physical borders. Non-profit organizations and agencies that are consistently looking for volunteers and funding are greatly assisted by these diverse learners as service providers. Students become assets to these agencies; they produce much needed workplace documents, such as memos, proposals, and newsletters, often in both English and Spanish. And students evince significant changes in identity as they write for these agencies.

Academically, as students learn to handle multiple discourses, their identities change from being academic writers addressing a professor to being professional writers in real workplace settings. Students discover for themselves what Gerald J. Alred refers to as different cultures, explaining how he found "a clear dividing line between works valued by academics and those valued by practitioners" (81). Veronica, for example, while enrolled in the bilingual writing practicum, reflects on her service-learning experience:

> Although many of the assignments were difficult to put together, I enjoyed writing for the 'real world.' I received a different satisfaction out of writing for an organization than I did when writing academically. The writing I did for the Nonprofit Enterprise Center made me feel like I was making a crucial difference in this organization. I feel like my articles and the newsletter…will help the Nonprofit Enterprise Center achieve its goal of changing the mentality many have of the nonprofit community.

Ernesto, feeling free to use his first language in the bilingual workplace writing course, reflected on his service-learning experience with Big Brothers Big Sisters of El Paso: "Aprendí que no es solor traducir, tal y como se lee, hay que traducir primero y luego darle sentido a toda nuestra traduccion y tal vez agregar palabras" (I learned that it's not only a matter of translating as it reads. You must translate first and then give the translation meaning and maybe even add words to it.)

Students' personal identities are also enhanced. They become civically engaged by helping meet their community's literacy needs, recognize the value of their native or second language, and appreciate their own and others' cultures by practicing intercultural communication, leading to professional growth. When students' languages are respected and appreciated, their self-esteem improves and they are more willing to experiment and take risks as communicators and language learners.

For instance, when Antonio entered the bilingual workplace writing course, he believed his writing skills in English, his second language, were weak. He opted to work with a community organization, and at the end of the semester, he shared with the class his conviction that his literacy skills in both languages had improved. Had he really improved as a writer? The documents he produced for Centro de Salud Familiar La Fe (a health clinic) demonstrate improvement, and this improvement not only shows in his class assignments but is also recognized in his agency mentor's end-of-semester evaluation. She says, "Antonio has a keen eye for copy editing and translation. He was a great help on several projects," and goes on to commend Antonio for his bilingualism, writing skills, dependability, and cultural sensitivity. Both the positive feedback and the opportunity to use his mother tongue to help others built Antonio's confidence and motivation to set higher standards for himself both in his community work and in his courses.

Adrian, a student in the same course who worked with the Hispanic Chamber of Commerce, expressed similar concerns at the beginning of the semester. His agency mentor stated, "Adrian has strong writing skills. He was in charge of writing memos, e-mails, and proofreading letters and our newsletter articles." Adrian, too, presented the documents he completed for the Chamber to the class at the end of the semester and expressed newfound confidence as a fluent, English-Spanish workplace writer and speaker. Students' reflections, agency mentors' profiles and evaluations, and progress reports from students on their service-learning each provides evidence that students are bridging borders, crossing regions, and building bridges while exploring and strengthening their own identities.

LOOKING AHEAD

It is important to document the long-term impact of this course. Studies are needed to understand the impact of students' writing in this course on the community. Longitudinal case studies would also be beneficial to determine what, if any, long-term transformational changes occur for the service-learning bilingual students. Richard Kiely's investigation of whether and how students were affected by their participation in an international service-learning program, documenting significant changes in political, moral, intellectual, personal, spiritual, and cultural orientations, provides one model for such a study. And, although no study has yet been conducted on the long term impact of UTEP's service-learning bilingual workplace writing course, based on students' reflections I venture to say that it changes career choices, and even job placement at the various non-profit organizations, are evidence of profound intellectual, personal, and/or cultural changes and transformations.

The service-learning workplace writing course I've described uses bilingualism and intercultural communication to bridge borders and strengthen students' identities. The course becomes a journey which may take the student, the agency mentor, and also the instructor to unexplored regions and often helps each of them to rediscover his or her origins, story, and purpose in society. The journey continues as the students move on beyond the course to fulfill roles as professionals and citizens engaged with their communities, society, and world.

WORKS CITED

Alred, Gerald J. "Bridging Cultures: The Academy and the Workplace." *Journal of Business Communication* 43.2 (2006): 79-88.

Bean, Janet et al. "Should We Invite Students to Write in Home Languages? Complicating the Yes/No Debate." *Second-Language Writing in the Composition Classroom: A Critical Sourcebook*. Eds. Paul Kei Matsuda, Michelle Cox, Jay Jordan, and Christina Ortmeier-Hooper. Boston and New York: Bedford/St. Martin's, 2006. 225-39.

Bowdon, Melody, and J. Blake Scott, *Service-Learning in Technical and Professional Communication*. New York: Longman, 2003.

Heilker, Paul. "Rhetoric Made Real: Civic Discourse and Writing Beyond the Curriculum." *Writing the Community: Concepts and Models for Service-Learning in Composition*. Eds. Linda Adler-Kassner, Robert Crooks, and Ann Watters. Washington, D.C.: AAHE, 1997. 71-77.

Kiely, Richard. "A Chameleon with a Complex: Searching for Transformation in International Service-Learning." *Michigan Journal of Community Service Learning* 10.2 (2004): 5-20.

National Commission on Writing for America's Families Schools and College. *The Neglected R.* New York: College Examination Board, 2003.

National Standards in Foreign Language Education Project. "Standards for Foreign Language Learning in the 21st Century." Lawrence, KS: Allen Press, 1999.

Rentz, Kathryn, and Ashley Mattingly. "Selling Peace in a Time of War: The Rhetorical and Ethical Challenges of a Graduate-Level Service-Learning Course." *Reflections* 4.2 (2004): 103-22.

Scenters-Zapico, John. "Tales from the U.S.-México Borderlands: Cultural Ecologies, Technology Gateways, and Sponsors of Literacies." CCCC Convention. Palmer House Hilton, Chicago. 23 Mar. 2006.

Stewart, Stuart. "Crossing Borders/Forging Identities: Echoes of Symbiosis between Classroom and Community." *Learning the Language of Global Citizenship: Service-Learning in Applied Linguistics.* Eds. Adrian Wurr and Josef Hellebrandt. Boston, MA: Anker Publishing, 2007. (in Press)

UTEP University Communications. UTEP FACTS 2005-2006. Sept. 2005.

Explore

What is service-learning? How does Baca use bilingualism with service-learning in her workplace writing course?

Invent

According to Baca, how can service-learning help students identify or rediscover their identity? Do you support service-learning as a college student? Why or why not? What are possible advantages and benefits of service-learning? What are possible disadvantages?

Collaborate

In small groups, discuss how service-learning can benefit students and non-profit organizations. In addition, identify the advantages of being bilingual when studying and/or working on the border.

Cartoons entertain, but can also teach lessons and/or mock political issues and politicians. Cartoons, such as the one below, while entertaining, reflect a perspective on immigration. With the construction of a border fence, more arguments and issues on immigration have risen in the United States.

STANDING FIRM

By Mark Hurwitt

What is the cartoon saying about immigration? What is Mark Hurwitt assuming about his audience?

In small groups, discuss how different forms of texts, such as cartoons, can present and support specific arguments and points of view. Give specific examples. Go to the internet and find different texts that support arguments or positions on immigration that you can identify and explain. These could include cartoons, pamphlets, brochures, websites, blogs, and others. Report your findings to the class.

Create a cartoon, billboard, or sign that presents your view on immigration. What are you assuming of your audience's knowledge, background, culture, language, education, nationality, and/or religious and political affiliations? Do an audience analysis and compose a profile of the audience for the text you create.

William T. Vollmann is a staff writer for The New York Times. *In his weekly Sunday book review column, Vollmann critiques* Crossers, *a book written by Philip Caputo. In this review, Vollmann states what he believes to be the moral of the book and expresses his view on the author's attempt to show people's conflicting feelings on illegal immigration.*

BORDERLANDS

BY WILLIAM T. VOLLMANN

A BOOK REVIEW OF *CROSSERS*

Once when I was so weak with amebic dysentery that all time not spent on the toilet was passed in bed, I found in my host's house one book in a language I could read. It was one of those storm-tossed but ultimately upbeat women's romances, a genre I had not yet sampled. I read it, then read it again and again, since there was nothing better to do. If I ever have the luxury of repeating such an experience, I hope to do so with a Philip Caputo book. For how many decades in how many used bookstores have I seen "Horn of Africa" standing steadfast, a Rock of Gibraltar compared with the mere boulders of Ken Follett and Sidney Sheldon? And only now, with a half-century of my life already over, have I finally learned whom to turn to for a good potboiler in my next wasting sickness!

The moral of "Crossers" is that the sins of the fathers are visited on the children, but not too much. (I will not give away the ending, but perhaps it would not be indiscreet to report that some good guys survive.) The setting is, mostly, the New Mexico-Arizona-México borderlands.

Caputo has stenciled his villains out of the cheapest cardboard he could find. The character of Yvonne, "queen of the city," the sadistic, nymphomaniacal, aging, addicted boss of a Mexican cartel, is about as convincing as Cruella De Vil. She snorts her "bumps of la puta blanca with a tiny gold spoon." Caputo reports the details of her decadent menus and describes the "glow in her cheeks" when sex has left her feeling younger. The other assassins, double agents et al., are less objectionable than simply formulaic; they would be equally at home in "The Day of the Jackal." That such people exist and commit their atrocities is indisputable, but why they do what they do is not something you will learn from this book. Accordingly, the plot of "Crossers" is as preposterous as that of any James Bond novel, which of course is not a bad thing if you like James Bond novels.

Where Caputo does succeed, and beautifully, is in portraying the conflicting feelings any thoughtful American has about illegal immigration. The San Ignacio ranch and its adjoining allotments constitute a rugged, wild stretch of the Old West, and the Anglo family who work it and consider it home would like to keep it more or less as it was. But transborder traffic flows through their property. Sometimes desperate girls, abandoned by their guides, come begging for water. Sometimes groups of crossers leave garbage and vandalize fences or water pipes. On one horrific occasion a van of illegals pursued by the Border Patrol comes crashing into a corral, killing or wounding many on board. What can one say about people who brave discomfort and extreme peril solely because, as one California Border Patrol officer once told me, "they do work most Americans won't do"? And what can one say to the residents of the San Ignacio ranch, who become, to say the least, tired of cleaning up the mess?

Blaine Erskine, paterfamilias of the San Ignacio, gets very, very tired indeed. His wife, Monica, remarks: "The wets"—wetbacks—"I guess I can put up with. But the coyotes and the drug mules—hideous people." And it is the drug mules and their employers whose menacing actions impel Blaine toward behavior that seems obsessive even to the vigilantes patrolling the border. "I had a talk with Blaine this morning, and maybe you should, too," one volunteer border guard tells a ranch visitor after Blaine fires warning shots dangerously close to some crossers. "That guy is getting a little spooky . . . Couldn't tell if they were wets or mules." The eventual result is a feud between Blaine and the villainous Yvonne, who has set up shop just across the border fence.

Blaine himself is convincingly drawn. Like his dead grandfather Ben, whose ghost haunts the narrative, he can be described as "a man who had outlived his time, only he didn't know it." The same may be true of the San Ignacio ranch itself.

Most of what we know about Ben derives from oral history transcripts in the archives of the Arizona Historical Society—a clever framing device on Caputo's part, allowing us to see Ben's brave, reckless, defiant and above all violent personality through a number of lenses. Blaine admires Ben's memory and is almost his reincarnation, right down to the coldly crooked smile that forebodes some punitive act. We look in on Ben in various remembered moments of his life: as the boy murderer of a Mexican who tried to rob him of his horse, as a young guerrilla and executioner during the Mexican Revolution, as a lawman who will stop at nothing to get his man, as a lawbreaker who will kidnap people and turn them over to their killers in order to pay a private debt of friendship, and finally, in old age, as a violent defender of his wife's honor.

Exactly how many of these episodes are familiar to Blaine we never find out, but we may be sure that he would approve of them all. Now that the frontier has been closed, Arizona granted statehood, police interrogators tamed by the Miranda rule and the rest of us intimidated by the Patriot Act, Blaine cannot be the old-style individualist that his grandfather was. His attempts in that direction merely enrage Yvonne more dangerously.

Why she is the enemy of Blaine's family in the first place is one of the book's secrets, but it may be safe to say that it has something to do with the many skeletons in Ben's closet. Caputo tells Ben's story with power and verisimilitude. His portrayal of the ranchers and their extended family also rings very true. He has a fine ear for Western dialogue, and these characters could almost be the ranchers I have met in my own part of the West.

But the real protagonist of the book, Blaine's cousin Gil Castle, is a New Yorker who goes "hunting on the veldts of the capital markets." Once his wife is killed in the Sept. 11 attacks, he takes early retirement and accepts an offer to hole up on Blaine's ranch while he tries to recover. Think of him as the most contemporary version of a type that always flourished in Zane Grey's westerns: the damaged, spoiled or effete Easterner who comes west, proves himself, finds love and puts down roots. It is ultimately Gil's moderation (not to mention his competence with an elephant gun out there on those financial veldts) that does the most to save the San Ignacio and the people on it. To me, this is a dispiriting and unconvincing lesson. I would rather see the San Ignacio people save themselves.

But the valuable quality Gil does represent is nuance. Unlike Blaine, he declines to applaud the Iraq war, feels uneasy about the growing Homeland Security detention apparatus, and hesitates to shoot at ambiguous Mexicans who lurk in odd corners of the ranch.

Gil, and through him the author, seeks eerie equations between Al Qaeda and drug cartels like Yvonne's, since both are terrorists. Once he even compares the American invasion of Iraq to the daily Mexican "invasions" of the United States border. I respect Caputo for considering these matters in his novel—and for not pushing his parallels too far. Ultimately Gil realizes there is no sanctuary here or in New York or anywhere, and that is just how life is. Indeed, the reason I enjoyed "Crossers" as much as I did (and I would have liked it better without Yvonne), is that it hints at how difficult it can be to draw conclusions—about evil, about Ben, and above all about the crossers themselves. "These people can drive you nuts," Monica says. "They break down your fences and break your heart, and you don't know what the hell to do about them."

According to Vollmann, Caputo does a good job of portraying the conflicting feelings any compassionate American has about illegal immigration. What are these feelings? Do you agree with Vollmann? Why or why not?

Go online and find another book review of *Crossers* by Philip Caputo. Summarize the second review and compare it with Vollmann's. Which review do you find more convincing? Why?

Find a book, an article, a movie, a song, or a poem on immigration or the borderlands. Write a review of it. Be sure to establish specific criteria to develop your evaluation. Use examples from the text you have selected to support your reasons for such an evaluation.

Jake Silverstein is editor of Texas Monthly, *a periodical that focuses on the beauty, sights, food, culture, and entertainment in the state of Texas. In the November 2010 issue, Silverstein addresses the U.S.-México border and immigration issues, particularly as they pertain to Texas. This is evident in his letter, as editor, of this* Texas Monthly *issue.*

POINT OF BORDER

BY JAKE SILVERSTEIN

The job of most editors, myself included, is to delight, entertain, surprise, and inform their readers. The majority of the time, when it comes to choosing a cover story, we try to keep the emphasis on the first three, since the other job of most editors, myself included, is to sell magazines. Then there are the months like this one. I'm not saying that a cover story on immigration won't sell—it's the hottest topic going right now, one that affects each and every one of us, one that instantly triggers strong feelings from all sides—but let's be honest, the fifty best burgers in Texas it ain't. Still, certain moments call for us to use our considerable energies—and our most precious real estate—for informative, ambitious, and civic-minded packages.

That the United States is now in the midst of yet another paroxysm of outrage over illegal immigration (and yet another paroxysm of outrage over the outrage) should be obvious to anyone with a television, a radio, or a high-speed Internet connection. Starting back in April, when Arizona governor Jan Brewer signed SB 1070, her state's controversial immigration bill, into law, we've been plunged into the latest round of an ugly debate that's plagued this nation since, well, the beginning. We're supposed to be a country of immigrants—huddled masses yearning to breathe free in a melting pot—but the truth is that we've always had a shut-the-door-behind-you mentality. No less a prototypical American than Benjamin Franklin was a true hard-liner on the subject of German immigration. "Why should Pennsylvania, founded by the *English*, become a Colony of Aliens," he wrote in 1751, "who will shortly be so numerous as to Germanize us instead of our Anglifying them, and will never adopt our Language or Customs." This distrust and skepticism of newcomers has persisted down through the centuries, and the various federal immigration laws we've passed (from 1924 to 1965 to 1986) have all had to wrestle with the deep paradox: We're a country of immigrants that's wary of newcomers.

Which may be why our process is so broken. Had we set out to create the most dysfunctional immigration system imaginable, it's unlikely that we could have done any better. It doesn't work for anyone (except, crucially, some employers), and it's created an enormous undocumented population—nearly 11 million people, according to the Department of Homeland Security—who live "in the shadows." Our basic strategy has been to ignore this situation entirely, even as we depend on the labor force it provides. Or at least that's our strategy until something disruptive happens, like a reform-minded president or a bad economy or a federal lawsuit challenging a state law, at which point all hell breaks loose. Twenty-two Arizona-style bills have now been introduced in state legislatures around the country. Clearly, avoiding the issue is no longer an option.

The resolution of all this is critically important to Texas, not only because at roughly 1.7 million our undocumented population is one of the highest in the country but because our history is so intertwined with immigration (legal and illegal, from many different countries, including, at one point, the United States). This is not an issue visited upon us from the outside. It's part of our culture. Yet like everyone else, we've too often let the discussion of immigration slide into the shadows too. It's a topic we'd just as soon avoid, one for which unanswered questions pile up and leave us misinformed about an increasingly fundamental aspect of the world we live in.

Which is why we decided to put together this issue, to surprise and inform (and maybe even entertain and delight here and there). And the discussion doesn't stop with these pages. On our website this month we're also launching a page dedicated to fostering discussion about immigration. You can find outtakes from the issue (photos, audio, and more), resources, and a place to post your thoughts. When it comes to fixing our screwed-up system, Texas can, and should, lead the way.

Silverstein states that it is important to address immigration in magazines and media of all sorts. Why does he feel this way? Do you agree or disagree with him? Why?

Silverstein believes Texas should lead the way when it comes to immigration reform. Why is Texas so important for this issue? If you do not reside in Texas, how do you view the role of your state (or specific city) in immigration reform?

Write an essay agreeing or disagreeing with Silverstein's statement: "We're a country of immigrants that's wary of newcomers." Support your position with examples and sources. Follow a specific documentation style for citing your sources (MLA or APA).

In the following transcript of a recorded conversation, Jake Silverstein presents a conversation among lawmakers and political figures, including himself, on different positions on immigration and border security. Silverstein begins with specific questions on the topic after a general greeting and chat on the guests' personal lives.

THE IMMIGRATION DINNER PARTY

By Jake Silverstein

What better place for strong conversation than over a meal? We gathered up lawmakers on both sides of the hottest debate going—plus a couple of experts—to break bread, argue, and see if any consensus could be reached by the time the dessert tray rolled around.

THE GUESTS

Rafael Anchía

Is a three-term Democratic state representative from West Dallas. He is an attorney specializing in public and corporate finance with the law firm of Haynes and Boone.

Leo Berman

Is a six-term Republican state representative from Tyler. He is a retired U.S. Army lieutenant colonel.

Richard Land

Has, since 1988, been the president of the Ethics and Religious Liberty Commission, the public-policy arm of the Southern Baptist Convention. He is from Houston.

Illustration by Steve Brodner

Steve Murdock

Is the former director of the U.S. Census Bureau and the former state demographer of Texas. He is a professor of sociology at Rice University.

Debbie Riddle

Is a four-term Republican state representative from North Harris County. She is a horse breeder.

Leticia Van de Putte

Is a five-term Democratic state senator from San Antonio and the former president of the National Hispanic Caucus of State Legislators. She is a pharmacist.

I. APPETIZERS

[*As the food arrives, the guests discuss their grandkids.*]

RIDDLE: Well, we just had our tenth grandbaby, and we've got them all right around us. I feel like the old woman who lived in the shoe.

BERMAN: You've got three more grandkids than I do, but I've got three great-grandsons.

VAN DE PUTTE: I always thought that grandparents were goofy, until I became one.

RIDDLE: And, you know, with each grandbaby you just get more obnoxious.

LAND: I was pretty much that way with my *kids*. My wife was praying that we would have another child before I totally ruined our eldest daughter. My name for her is Princess Jennifer Rebekah Sweetheart Supergirl. She wanted a tiara for her fifth birthday.

RIDDLE: Did she get one?

LAND: She did.

BERMAN: I've gone through three tiaras.

RIDDLE: I feel very lucky. All of our children live very close. One's five minutes around the corner one way; the other's five minutes around the corner the other way. And my mother lives just a few houses down.

VAN DE PUTTE: I hate to tell you this, Debbie, but you're Hispanic.

RIDDLE: I think you're right. [*laughter*]

JAKE SILVERSTEIN, EDITOR, *Texas Monthly*: We're here tonight to talk about illegal immigration, immigration reform, and border security. And, Representative Berman, I thought we'd begin with you. We know that right now there are anywhere from 10 million to 12 million undocumented immigrants in the country and somewhere around 1.4 million in the state of Texas. So here's a simple question to get us started: How serious a challenge do we face from that population?

BERMAN: I want to disagree with the numbers you have. The numbers that I see are that we have no less than twenty million illegal aliens in the United States today and two and a half million in Texas. They come here because we've done absolutely nothing, zero, about illegal aliens in Texas. In 2006 the Lone Star Foundation did a comprehensive study that said we're spending $5 billion a year to take care of illegal aliens in Texas. Incarceration alone is, like, $42 million. Plus, the doctors will tell you that we're treating illegal aliens for a number of diseases, many that we normally don't even treat anymore because we've had drugs to wipe them out. And children of illegal aliens make up about 15 percent of every school district—that's a rough average across the 1,200 districts. So if you take 15 percent of the total bond packages that schools are trying to pass in Texas to build new school buildings, 15 percent of those buildings are for the children of illegal immigrants, who are not paying property taxes.

MURDOCK: Let me say a little bit about the numbers, because that's what I do for a living. First of all, all of the groups that I know—this includes left and right—that have done their academic research on this would argue that the number is between 10 and 12 million, not 20. Whether you talk about Homeland Security or the Pew Hispanic Center or the Center for Immigration Reform, all of those are in that ballpark for the country and all of them are somewhere between 1.4 and 1.7 million for Texas, and nearly all of them, frankly, agree that since 2007 there's been either a decline in the numbers or at least stability.

LAND: Is that nationally, statewide, or both?

MURDOCK: Both. Now, to look at the impact of immigrants, you basically have to separate it by level. The reality is that most immigrants are employed by large employers, and they do pay Social Security. They do pay income tax. It's taken off their checks just like it's taken off mine. If someone has a false Social Security card and pays Social Security, Social Security doesn't say, "Oh, I need to find out who this is and send it back." They keep that money, and some of us who are getting older may appreciate having that money someday in the Social Security trust fund. One of the last few times Alan Greenspan appeared before Congress, he was asked what would help Social Security, and the second thing he mentioned was more immigration, because, he said, immigrants are paying in and not taking out. So if you look at that, they're a net positive at the national level. At the state level most studies suggest that it's about a wash. At the local level they may be somewhat negative because of education costs and health costs, which are all locally incurred.

ANCHÍA: The numbers my friend and colleague Representative Berman alludes to are numbers that I've not seen in official studies, so let's look at a study from 2006 from then Republican comptroller Carole Keeton Strayhorn. She did a comprehensive study, not just on the cost side but the benefit side. I'll use back-of-the-napkin round numbers, but the state benefit in terms of revenue was about $450 million. Again, these are round numbers. The local impact cost was about $950 million, leaving about a $500 million delta between cost and benefit, state and local. Then she went a step further and looked at the economic value of our immigrants in Texas, and she came up with what I think was a pretty conservative figure of $17.7 billion of economic value. I'm a corporate finance lawyer by trade, and I represent some of the most sophisticated financial professionals and clients in the state. If I ever offered the opportunity to them to invest $500 million to receive a $17.7 billion return, they would take that deal all day long.

BERMAN: Well, the biggest problem in my area, in East Texas, is the fact that illegal aliens are going into the wrecker business, and they're undercutting the people in my district by half. And so those people can't put new people to work because they're not making any money. I received a note from my maid that said, "Mr. Berman, my income from last year to support my two daughters is half of what it used to be because I'm being undercut by illegal aliens who are actually cleaning houses at far more capacity than I can possibly do, so I'm being cut out of a lot of jobs myself."

VAN DE PUTTE: I would agree that there are costs. But even if we take Leo's number of two and a half million, that means, what, a tenth of our population? My leadership in this state can't have it both ways. They can't beat their chests and yell out loud that we've got the strongest economy in the country and then say we have an immigration problem. The response of rational people should be, if you're here to work, if you're here to contribute, bring it on. And if you're here to sell my daughter drugs, then you're going to be held accountable, regardless of your status.

RIDDLE: Yes, the people in my district are very concerned about that. Illegal immigration is probably the number one priority for people in my district. They've stopped asking for border security—they're demanding border security. Let me share with you some numbers. In Houston, since 2004, we have had a 71 percent increase in the number of gangs and a 250 percent increase in gang-related crimes. This is all connected with the drug cartels. These gangs are incredibly sophisticated, they have the automatic weapons, they have night-vision goggles, and they have the chase cars. The drug cartels have a $25-billion-a-year cash profit. They are going to do whatever it takes, and the crimes are serious. We live in a post-9/11 world. It is now altogether possible to put a dirty

International bridge between El Paso and Ciudad Juárez

bomb in a suitcase and walk across the border and go into downtown Houston, detonate it, and kill a million people. I have asked folks, "Do you lock your doors at night when you go to bed?" And I bet everyone around this table would say yes. The reason you lock your doors at night is to make sure that you have no intruders. To make sure that your family is safe. To make sure that your home is secure. The people of this state and the people of this nation deserve to go to bed at night knowing that our border is safe and that we're not just letting a criminal element come over for whatever reason. We're either a nation of laws or we're not. We either have a border or we don't.

II. ENTRÉES

SILVERSTEIN: Dr. Land, let's turn to the question of reform. Most of your work on this issue has been at the federal level, and as we know, that's where the big fixes are. In your view, what are the next steps?

LAND: This issue has reached a critical mass of urgency. I think it's rending the social fabric of the nation. And the support for the Arizona law in other states is indicative of that. It's been fifty years since we've had an administration that seriously enforced the border or internal immigration laws. Let's be honest, we've had two signs up at the border for the past thirty years. One says "No trespassing" and the other one says "Help wanted." And we have not enforced our laws internally. We've had people who have been here twenty years or more. And they have worked here, they have married citizens, they have produced citizens, and their assimilation has been retarded by a lot of lousy immigration laws. If they had been able to be documented, they wouldn't have been as exploited, they wouldn't have been as fearful of the law, they would have already been assimilating. I don't think that the language issue is an issue. Most Hispanics understand that if they want to assimilate, they need to learn English. I grew up in Houston. Twenty-five or so kids in my high school were Hispanic, and a lot of them were in Spanish class with me, trying to learn Spanish. We've made this problem worse. It's been greatly exacerbated by the fact that we haven't had a federal administration that has seriously enforced the immigration laws since Eisenhower.

RIDDLE: Republican *or* Democrat.

LAND: That's right. So I don't think we can secure the southern border now without having immigration reform that says, number one, beyond a certain date, if you want to have a job in the United States, you have to have a guest-worker card that is biometric and tamperproof. And if you're an American citizen, you have to have a Social Security card that has been reissued with your thumbprint on it. If they can't get a job once they get here, they're not going to come. That makes the border secure. And then I would argue that we need to have a six-month period under which people who are undocumented can come forward; undergo a background check; agree to get one of these guest-worker cards; pay fines; agree to learn to read, write, and speak English; pass a test saying that they've done so; and go to the back of the line, behind those who have been trying to come here legally. I think that that'd probably take ten years. What I'm arguing for is a grand compromise that would pass one piece of legislation, but it would be implemented sequentially, not simultaneously.

SILVERSTEIN: And securing the border comes first?

LAND: The government would have to have certain agreed-upon metrics for determining that the border is secure, and then Congress would have to certify that they have been met. Then it would trigger the second part.

SILVERSTEIN: Which says what?

LAND: You pass a law that says that anyone who employs anyone who does not have one of those biometric cards goes to jail for a year. I was on the Council on Foreign Relations task force, and we estimated, based on the studies we saw, that this would increase the wages at the lower tier of the economy by about 10 percent. Which is a big increase for those folks. Now, the other thing we discovered when we did this task force was that only about 70 percent of undocumented people want to stay here permanently. If we had a real guest-worker program, with a border that actually worked, they would come here, make money, and then go back and start a garage in Monterrey.

ANCHÍA: But if they did stay in the program, they could get full legal status?

LAND: Yes. If you don't break the law.

BERMAN: Now, Richard, what does "full legal status" mean? Does it mean amnesty with a pathway to citizenship?

LAND: No one's talking about amnesty. Amnesty is what Jimmy Carter gave those who avoided service during the Vietnam War. I'm talking about a fine, and I'm talking about a background check, and I'm talking about learning to read, write, and speak English. I'm talking about going to the back of the line, where they would pay the penalty of having to wait behind those who are trying to come here legally.

RIDDLE: There are situations that I think we all have in our districts where we have someone who's 87 years old who came here illegally but she's been here. There's no one with a lick of sense who would send that 87-year-old woman back or make her go through a great deal of aggravation to become legal. An overall broad-sweeping amnesty I don't think can work, nor would I think the

American people would allow it, but there are situations at the opposite end of the spectrum, like having a young person who was brought over here as an infant and has grown up in America and is American and may not even know the language of México or any other country.

ANCHÍA: Canada.

RIDDLE: But we've got to look at the crime, the gangs, the drug cartels, the human smuggling, everything that is coming across our border. It's hitting Texas really hard.

SILVERSTEIN: Leo, what do you disagree with in that version of comprehensive reform?

BERMAN: Well, I'd like to make several comments about what Richard just said. I'm a first-generation American. I've been here for 75 years. My parents came from Europe, through Ellis Island. I am totally supportive of legal immigration into the United States. But one problem that I see happening in the United States right now is the fact that we are denigrating our citizenship. We're giving citizenships to children of individuals who are committing a crime against the United States, children who were born of illegal people here in the United States. I would like to see that stopped.

LAND: I would agree that we need to stop it, but the way to stop it is not to change the Fourteenth Amendment.

BERMAN: The Fourteenth Amendment was ratified in 1868 to ensure that the children of former slaves were indeed U.S. citizens if born in the United States.

VAN DE PUTTE: I want to disagree. The Fourteenth Amendment says any person born or *naturalized* in the United States or subject to its jurisdiction is considered a citizen of the United States. The term "naturalized" wasn't just for slaves.

BERMAN: After we pass a bill at the Legislature, we always ask each other questions to get legislative intent. Well, they get senatorial intent too. And in 1866 an author of the Fourteenth Amendment, Senator Jacob Howard, from Michigan, said on the floor of the United States Senate that this does not apply to foreigners, it does not apply to ambassadors, it does not apply to diplomats coming through the United States. Why would the Russian ambassador come to the United States and have a child and want that child to be a U.S. citizen?

LAND: Well, he would be disqualified because he's not subject to the jurisdiction of the laws of the United States.

BERMAN: Neither are illegal aliens subject to the jurisdiction thereof.

LAND: Well, they are.

BERMAN: No, they're not.

LAND: Sure they are.

BERMAN: Ask yourself three questions. If they're subject to the jurisdiction of the United States, can they be called to jury duty? Can they vote? Does an eighteen-year-old alien, whether legal or illegal—

ANCHÍA: But legal permanent residents can't do those three things, and they're subject to the jurisdiction of the United States. If the litmus test is jury duty, legal permanent residents aren't called to jury duty, and neither are seventeen-year-olds, right?

BERMAN: I'm talking about illegal aliens. I'm talking about aliens here on a visa. I served in the military for 22 years. I was in combat for 2 years, and I've always valued my citizenship more than anything else that I've got. And we're making a mockery of citizenship when we give citizenship to the children of parents who are violating our law at the time and when we give citizenship to people who can buy it for $5,000.

LAND: But that would be like if the president of the United States sent me a notice and it said, "You know, we have been tracking your speeding habits on the interstate for the past twenty-six years. And we've documented every time you've exceeded the speed limit. And now we're going to send you a ticket for every time you broke the speed limit for the last twenty-six years. And we're going to confiscate your car." Well, I think that's unfair. For 26 years we have ignored our own laws. And I think it's unfair to now, all of the sudden, say we're going to enforce those laws retroactively.

RIDDLE: I don't think he's talking about retroactively.

BERMAN: I'm not talking about retroactive. It's not retroactive at all.

LAND: Anyway, if we have a comprehensive immigration reform law that worked, this would be a moot point.

BERMAN: Why?

LAND: Because we wouldn't have undocumented people working here and having babies here. They would all be documented.

BERMAN: Well, what about the legal ones who are buying it for $5,000?

ANCHÍA: That's an enforcement issue. That's training your port-of-entry guards that under current law they have the discretion to turn away pregnant women at any port of entry on a visa basis.

MURDOCK: Can I suggest something? Before we decide that this is a problem, let's find out how many people it really is.

BERMAN: The number that I got is 300,000 a year. Total illegal and tourist, 300,000 a year. And 63,000 illegal citizenships here in Texas.

ANCHÍA: You're incorrect on that, actually. Because that 63,000 figure, just so everybody is reporting it correctly, that was an article done by the *Dallas Morning News*, and it only bears out that there are 63,000 children born to *noncitizens*. They could be visa holders, legal permanent residents—both of whom are here legally—or undocumented.

MURDOCK: Most of that 300,000 comes from people who have lived here many years and have babies like everybody does at certain life stages. They came here to work, and they got involved in life.

RIDDLE: So you're saying that it's just a total myth that people cross our borders to have a baby?

MURDOCK: I'm saying that the numbers get inflated.

RIDDLE: I'm not talking about numbers. Do you think that there is a significant—you're a statistician. I'm not asking for—

MURDOCK: Yeah, I can answer that. It is not a significant number, given the population and given the total births in the United States.

RIDDLE: What about Texas?

MURDOCK: For Texas too. Now, are there large numbers from people who are not technically legal? Yes. But that's different from saying people are just coming over here to give birth.

BERMAN: I'm going to have to challenge that also, because at Parkland Hospital, in Dallas, 70 percent of the births are to illegal aliens.

ANCHÍA: No, to *noncitizens*.

BERMAN: But where do they come from, Rafael?

VAN DE PUTTE: They've *been* here, Leo. They've been here since they were two years old. They've gone to school, and now they're getting married and stuff, but they've *been* here.

BERMAN: Are they legal or illegal?

ANCHÍA: They're mixed. There's some who are here on visas, some who are legal permanent residents, and there's some who are undocumented.

VAN DE PUTTE: What you're assuming is that everybody who's a noncitizen is not legal, and that's absolutely false.

BERMAN: I think I'm pretty close, really. I think I'm very close.

III. DESSERT

SILVERSTEIN: Let's talk about the border and whether it can be secured, since that's clearly a critical part of any reform package.

RIDDLE: Well, I asked Colonel [Steve] McCraw, the director of the Department of Public Safety, "Is our border secure?" He said, "Absolutely not." So I asked, "Can it be secured?" And he said yes. Privately I asked him, "What is your definition of a secure border?" And the answer was that not one person cross our border that we're not aware of. That not one person cross over illegally.

ANCHÍA: That's a pretty high bar. If the discussion on comprehensive immigration reform can't happen until your definition is met, then it will never happen.

RIDDLE: No, it has got to happen.

VAN DE PUTTE: Well, let me ask you something. I got to spend a couple days with Border Patrol in the Nogales area. And at the end of one day we went into the detention area, and they had almost five hundred people in cages. A lot were children and women and families. And then, over to one side, there was a cage with about twenty guys in there. And the border chief was talking to us, and what he said was basically, "Ladies, I can spend my five hundred agents trying to catch these people over here who want to take care of your kids. They want to work, they want to do your lawn, they want to put on a roof. Or I can use my manpower to catch these men who want to sell your daughters drugs. I can't do both. And the policymakers have to set the priority."

RIDDLE: I absolutely don't disagree with you. But that doesn't mean we should not secure the border. What you're talking about is not checking criminal background, not checking—

VAN DE PUTTE: No, what I'm talking about is setting priorities. Unfortunately, our federal government has not set those priorities. They give equal weight to the sixteen-year-old who's crossing who wants to clean somebody's house and the guy who's carrying kilos.

LAND: I don't think a 100 percent seal is realistic, but we've got to substantially seal it. How do you do that? Well, I think we're going to have to have more border agents, but once you have a way for people to come legally and you have a way to stop people from being employed illegally on this side of the border, then the pressure on the border slackens.

RIDDLE: And I think you're absolutely right.

LAND: And then you go after the criminals. I have a couple of reasons for this sense of urgency. One is because I think the Arizona law and the response to it shows that we have reached a sort of critical mass of rending the social structure. Secondly, President [Felipe] Calderón may be the best president of México the United States is ever going to have. We have a vested interest in him succeeding, because if he fails, I'm very fearful that we're either going to have a drug lord running the country or we're going to have someone like [Hugo] Chávez running the country, and that's going to be very, very, very serious, because then we're going to have refugees like we have with Cuba. And we're not going to turn those folks away.

SILVERSTEIN: So let's talk about the Arizona law. Obviously this looms over our discussion, not only SB 1070 but the Obama administration's response to it.

LAND: I don't support either one.

BERMAN: Neither one? Why don't you support SB 1070?

LAND: I think it puts law enforcement officials in an untenable situation. And it's going to let some bad actors get off, because they're going to be arrested for legitimate reasons like drug trafficking and they're going to claim they were racially profiled. The way to handle the Arizona law and the situation with Arizona is not by suing Arizona but by passing federal comprehensive regulation that makes the Arizona law irrelevant. Now, I understand why SB 1070 was passed. It was passed because Arizona was desperate.

SILVERSTEIN: Leo, you've indicated that you intend to introduce legislation similar to SB 1070 in the next session. Why do you think this legislation is good for Texas?

BERMAN: There's three major parts of my bill. The first part of the bill has to do with local law enforcement dealing directly with illegal aliens in the United States. But I struck two sentences out of the first part of the Arizona bill, which will do away with profiling completely. The bill that I'm introducing has nothing to do with profiling. The second part outlaws sanctuary cities. The third part requires all employers to use the E-Verify system.

SILVERSTEIN: How does your language avoid profiling?

BERMAN: I took out the sentences in the first part of the bill that give the local law enforcement discretion. They ask everybody. Everybody they stop is asked the same thing.

VAN DE PUTTE: What about papers? Leo, would you have everyone carry papers?

BERMAN: No, a driver's license, a registration of the car, an insurance policy. You have to show that you're a U.S. citizen.

ANCHÍA: How do you prove that?

BERMAN: Driver's license.

ANCHÍA: That doesn't prove that. Legal permanent residents, visa holders—all have driver's licenses.

BERMAN: But they're legally in the United States.

ANCHÍA: What if they speak Spanish? Is that probable cause?

BERMAN: No.

VAN DE PUTTE: What really worried me was, in preparation for the Arizona law, we had Catholic priests who were telling their parishioners, "Take your saints off of your car. Take the Lady of Guadalupe off. Take off all religious stuff. Do not wear a crucifix."

BERMAN: I'm not filing that bill, Leticia.

VAN DE PUTTE: But what I'm telling you is, when folks think about Arizona, maybe they're not thinking about what has been struck down. I've got to tell you, part of me is very excited there is an Arizona law, because I don't think our federal government would have even begun the discussion unless they thought there'd be fifty different Arizona state laws. And on the other side, I really think that there are those in my Democratic party who just love every time you [to Berman] open your mouth or you [to Riddle] open your mouth.

BERMAN: Why? Because we're not going to get the Latino votes? That's what you're telling me? I wish I could show you the stack of letters that I got concerning not only that bill but English as the official language of Texas and the number of Hispanics who have written to me saying, "Thank you for doing this." I've gotten hundreds of letters from Hispanics. They're not all against this.

SILVERSTEIN: Richard, let me ask you about the role of faith in this debate. How does the Southern Baptist Convention get to its position on immigration reform?

LAND: My role is to call Southern Baptists to be where I believe Southern Baptists ought to be based on our understanding of Christianity, so that's what I've been trying to do. During the 2006 immigration debate, Southern Baptists came together for our annual meeting, and we overwhelmingly passed a resolution that called for enforcing the border first and called for a fair and just path to legal status for those who were here in an undocumented sense.

RIDDLE: And I think my pastor is supporting you, right?

LAND: He is, and my position has helped him to come to an understanding, because he's got, what, 1,500 Hispanics in his church? To me it's a moral issue. I had the privilege to lead the Southern Baptist Convention in 1995 to apologize for having supported slavery and racism. We had passed twenty-something resolutions condemning racism since 1946, but we'd never apologized and we'd never taken personal responsibility, and when we did that, it lanced the boil. At the time, there were 335,000 African American Southern Baptists. Today there are a million. So that's a 300 percent increase in fifteen years. And I did ask the question at our annual convention this summer in Orlando. I said, "How much more successful would we have been at evangelizing African Americans had we adopted the integrationist stance in the sixties that my commission asked us to do at the time?" I don't want to have to come back in fifteen years and apologize to Hispanics for having supported anti-Hispanic immigration rhetoric.

BERMAN: Anti-Hispanic immigration rhetoric? Is that what we're supporting, anti-Hispanic—

LAND: I didn't say you were. I'm talking about what's happening at the national level. I'm talking about what's happening in the Congress.

BERMAN: Are we a nation of laws or are we not a nation of laws?

LAND: Well, we've been a nation that has ignored our laws.

BERMAN: When I started in office, I took the same oath that everyone else does, to preserve and protect and defend the Constitution and laws of the United States.

LAND: We have to bear some responsibility, as a nation, for having allowed our government to ignore our laws for so many years and the consequences that come with that.

Go online and do a "search" on one of the participants in the conversation. What overall picture do you get of this person?

In a small group, have a conversation on immigration and border security. Record the group's main points and arguments in the conversation. Present the summary of your conversation to the class.

Select one of the participants from the immigration dinner party. Write a profile of this individual. Describe his/her political, educational, and professional background. State and explain this individual's position on immigration and border security.

Michele Waslin is the Senior Policy Analyst at the Immigration Policy Center in the U.S. She holds a Ph.D., and she contributed this article in 2009 through Immigration Impact. For the complete story, go to http://www.alternet.org/bloggers/http://immigrationimpact.com//141300/

LARGE IMMIGRANT POPULATIONS MAKE CITIES SAFE...JUST ASK EL PASO

BY MICHELE WASLIN

El Paso, Texas, is a relatively poor, Hispanic, gun-friendly city and home to many undocumented immigrants. Yet although El Paso is adjacent to a violence-riddled Mexican city, it's actually counted among the safest big cities in the U.S. Why is El Paso so safe? A recent article in *Reason Online* dispels some of the myths associated with immigrants and crime.

Many Americans believe that immigrants—especially illegal immigrants—are associated with high levels of crime. However, according to criminologist Jack Levin, El Paso is safe *because* of its immigrant population.

If you want to find a safe city, first determine the size of the immigrant population. If the immigrant community represents a large proportion of the population, you're likely in one of the country's safer cities. San Diego, Laredo, El Paso—these cities are teeming with immigrants, and they're some of the safest places in the country.

The Immigration Policy Center (IPC) has repeatedly provided factual information about the lack of relationship between immigrants and crime levels.

- Although the undocumented immigrant population doubled to about 12 million from 1994 to 2004, data from the Bureau of Justice Statistics indicates that the violent crime rate in the United States declined by 35.1 percent during this time and the property crime rate fell by 25.0 percent.

- According to a 2008 report from the conservative Americas Majority Foundation, crime rates are lowest in states with the highest immigration growth rates. From 1999 to 2006, the total crime rate declined 13.6 percent in the 19 highest-immigration states, compared to a 7.1 percent decline in the other 32 states. In 2006, the 10 "high influx" states—those with the most dramatic, recent increases in immigration—had the lowest rates of violent crime and total crime.

Yet the myth persists—due, in part, to news headlines that read, "Hispanic males are now majority in county jails," which appeared in the *Arizona Republic* this week.

Caution Traffic Sign—Crossing Of Immigrants

Not surprisingly, the number of Hispanic males in Maricopa County jails has increased recently due to Sheriff Joe Arpaio's mission to incarcerate as many immigrants as possible. Arpaio conducts immigration sweeps as part of his partnership with the Department of Homeland Security to enforce federal immigration laws. This, in conjunction with new laws that allow undocumented immigrants to be charged with conspiracy to smuggle themselves and denying them bail, all add up to large numbers of immigrants in jail.

Just because immigrants are in jail, doesn't mean that they are criminals. Just like in Maricopa County, the number of immigrants in jail for immigration violations and who have never been convicted of a crime is increasing. The Pew Hispanic Center recently reported that in 2007, immigration offenses represented nearly one-quarter of all federal convictions, up from just 7 percent in 1991. It is telling that 61 percent of the non-U.S. citizen Latino immigrants sentenced in federal courts in 2007 were sentenced for immigration offenses, not violent crimes or theft.

Everyone agrees that violent criminals and threats to our community should be prioritized. But the fact is that immigrants, including undocumented immigrants, are actually less likely to commit crimes than U.S. citizens.

We must ask ourselves whether spending large amounts of resources arresting, detaining, prosecuting, and deporting immigrants who have no criminal background is really the best use of time and money—resources that could be used to pursue real criminals. Enacting comprehensive immigration reform that includes a legalization program is a much more efficient and effective way to bring unauthorized immigrants out of the shadows and ensure that they live and work legally in the U.S.

According to Waslin, what myths exist about immigrants and crime? Why is El Paso, Texas one of the safest cities in the U.S.?

Using immigrant population as the criterion, how safe is the city you live in? What is your city's immigrant population? How do you feel about this number?

Write an essay evaluating how safe your city is. Include immigrant population as one of the criteria to determine safety and security. You can agree or disagree with Waslin's use of immigrant population to show safety or danger in your city. Provide support for your evaluation and reasons.

Through its website, texasmonthly.com, Texas Monthly conducted an interview with Latino journalist, Jorge Ramos. The interview focuses on Ramos's book Dying to Cross, *where Ramos describes and discusses a horrible immigrant tragedy in American history. In this interview, Ramos also discusses his efforts as an immigration reform advocate.*

COMING TO AMERICA:
AN INTERVIEW WITH JORGE RAMOS

By Texasmonthly.com

Television journalist Jorge Ramos, the author of the book Dying to Cross, *on immigration reform and being called the "voice of the voiceless."*

A brief numerical synopsis of Jorge Ramos' successful journalism career reads something like this: five wars covered, seven books written, seven Emmy awards won, and nineteen years as lead anchor for *Noticiero Univision*, a nightly news show watched by approximately 98 percent of the 40 million Spanish households in the United States. All of this, plus a daily radio commentary and weekly newspaper column, by the young age of 47.

Ramos is many things to the U.S. Hispanic community, most certainly a household name: The *Miami Herald* says he's "bigger than Peter Jennings, Dan Rather and Tom Brokaw" because his newscast ratings consistently trump all other networks in Miami, San Francisco, and Houston. He's as influential as Oprah: The book club he started in 2002 regularly catapults his three monthly recommendations into Spanish-language best-sellers. He's the face of a changing nation: Ramos came to the United States from México with a

Author, Jorge Ramos

student visa in 1983, and his own immigrant experience has focused his reportorial eye on the plight of what he calls the country's "second wave" of immigrants.

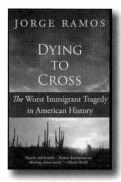

In his latest book, *Dying to Cross* (excerpted in *Texas Monthly*'s pages this month), Ramos recounts the "worst immigrant tragedy in American history"—the harrowing tale of the deaths of nineteen Mexican immigrants crammed into a sweltering truck trailer that was abandoned near Victoria, Texas.

texasmonthly.com: Tell me about the book. How long did you work on it? How many interviews did you conduct?

Jorge Ramos: The book actually started with a television program that we did about a year and a half ago, and through the program, I had the opportunity to interview many of the survivors of this tragedy, including the mother of the five-year-old who died in the truck. I had direct access to many of the people who actually lived through the agony of being in the truck for those four hours, but also with many of the politicians involved in the investigation and some of the families who learned later on that their husbands and brothers and friends had died.

texasmonthly.com: Were they open to talking? Were any hesitant to talk to you?

JR: All of the survivors were undocumented immigrants—though the U.S. government has granted them residency while the trials go on—and right at the beginning they were very reluctant and afraid of speaking to anyone, officials or reporters, because they didn't know what was going to happen to their immigration status. But after that was resolved, they were very open in telling me, in detail, what they went through during those four hours and how they got into the U.S. Mostly I talked with four of them who were not only willing to talk to me at length about what happened but were also willing to go back to a truck that was exactly like the one they were in and relive with me for the television program and for the book their experience. That was a shocking, dramatic experience because they had no idea how difficult it was going to be for them to relive what they went through.

texasmonthly.com: What spurred you on to investigate this particular tragedy?

JR: The most important thing to remember is that this is one of the worst tragedies involving immigrants ever to happen in the U.S. Never in the past has there been nineteen immigrants who've died in a tragedy like this. It set a precedent. And we have never seen an investigation in which the U.S. government has looked for the death penalty for some of those implicated in this [type of] crime. It seems that the U.S. government wanted to make an example of this case. They looked for the coyotes, or human traffickers, in ways in which I've never seen before—no expenses were spared and many of them were even found in México. Thirdly, and very importantly, this case highlights the tragedy of undocumented immigrants coming to this country and dying. Every single day on average one immigrant dies at the border, so every year we have between 350 and 400 immigrants dying at the border, trying to cross.

It is much more difficult to cross the border because of new security measures put in place after 9/11; however, every single day on average 1,300 immigrants cross the border illegally from México into the U.S. and stay in the U.S., so for them they are betting on this cruel statistic that only one out of 1,300 [immigrants] dies at the border, and that's why they keep on trying. I just read a report released by the Pew Hispanic Center that stated as of March 2005, the undocumented population is approaching 11 million people and nearly 6 million are Mexican. Right now there's chaos at the border—the border is not under control, people are dying at the border. It doesn't matter if you're for the immigrants or you have an anti-immigrant position. What's important is that something has to be done at the border, and I think this book highlights the tragedy that goes on but also makes the case that something has to be done between the U.S. and México. Unless there is an immigration agreement between México and the U.S. and unless we have a more orderly flow of immigrants coming into the U.S., this tragedy will keep on repeating every nineteen days.

texasmonthly.com: What's the best-case scenario for immigration reform?

JR: The best-case scenario includes three measures. First, there has to be an immigration agreement between México and the U.S. to have a more orderly flow of immigrants coming to the U.S.—immigrants who, by the way, are needed in this country. Number two, there has to be a comprehensive immigration agreement to legalize and to identify the 11 million undocumented immigrants living in this country. Third, there has to be an investment—a huge investment program—in Latin America so that people living in those countries can stay in their own countries without having to come to the U.S. to find a job. Those are the three most important measures to take to create order and keep the border under control, otherwise we will keep on having immigrants crossing the border illegally, immigrants dying at the border, and even anti-immigrant groups trying to take justice into their own hands.

texasmonthly.com: How would you explain to a person born and raised in the U.S. what it feels like to be an immigrant? What drives a person to want to flee his country so badly that he'll take such a deadly risk?

JR: There's a lot of misinformation about immigrants in this country, and it's very un-American to criticize new immigrants and to forget that most of our families were also immigrants. It is important to emphasize that all immigrants, both legal and undocumented, contribute up to $10 billion to the country every single year according to the National Academy of Sciences (a prestigious group of distinguished science and engineering scholars in the U.S.). In other words, immigrants contribute much more to the economy of this country, to this culture, and to this society, than what they take away from it. We tend to forget these things. We have to take a second look at immigration in this country. Since 9/11 many people are very sensitive to the fact that our border is not under control, but we also have to remember that not a single one of the terrorists involved in 9/11 crossed the border illegally from México and that those terrorists have absolutely nothing to do with the 11 million undocumented immigrants in this country whose only objective is to find a job and get a better life.

texasmonthly.com: Shifting a bit to your own experiences in this country: You are an anchorman and a best-selling author, and you write a weekly column and have a daily radio commentary. How do you do it all?

JR: You just have to be very organized, and that's what I do. I try to write and do my radio commentaries every morning after I drop my sons off, so I usually write from 9 [a.m.] to 11 [a.m.], and I try to exercise before that if I can. After that I spend most of my day at the television station. I still need to exercise to try to get a clear mind, so I play soccer every Saturday morning, which is like a ritual, and on other days of the week, I try to jog, play tennis, and I've just discovered yoga—so maybe that helps me.

texasmonthly.com: What drives you to maintain such a demanding schedule?

JR: Even though I've been living in this country for more than twenty years, I still feel like an immigrant. I am an immigrant, and I feel that I have a responsibility to voice the concerns of those immigrants who don't have a voice in this country. That's what drives me professionally, not only to be an objective reporter or anchorman every single day, but also when I can—and I can when I write my articles and give my opinion on radio—to try to explain to those who do not understand the immigrant experience what it is to be an immigrant in this country. So in a way I am trying to be a bridge between those of us who are immigrants and those of us who are not.

texasmonthly.com: You've been called the "voice of the voiceless." Why is that important to you?

JR: It is not something that I chose to be, but as a journalist and as a writer, I have a responsibility, as many other Latino authors and journalists have, to represent our country and try to explain to those who are not Latinos or immigrants what it means to be Hispanic in this country. Also we have to understand that the U.S. is becoming a more diversified country. Latinos will become the majority in this country by mid-century. We won't be here to live it and experience it, but Latinos will eventually, because of a demographic revolution, become the majority. Latinos are already the majority in cities like Miami and San Antonio, and eventually Latinos will become the majority in states like California and Texas. This process of transformation is well under way, and the U.S. sometimes does not realize that this process of transformation is changing everything: It's what I call the Latinization of the U.S. It's changing the way we work, the way we speak—already the U.S. follows closely behind México, Spain, and Argentina as the largest Spanish-speaking country in the world—so we have to be aware that this country is changing, for the best I think. It is more diversified than ever before, and we have to be prepared for that change.

Explore

According to the interview, what does Ramos see as the best form of immigration reform? Do you agree or disagree with Ramos? Why?

Invent

How is Ramos "the voice of the voiceless?" Point out specific examples from the interview that support your answer. Do you see Ramos as "the voice of the voiceless?" Why or why not?

Compose

Conduct an interview with an immigrant or immigration expert. List your interview questions ahead of time. Define the purpose for your interview. You may record the interview (but request the interviewee's permission first), transcribe it, and present it in Question & Answer format as in the interview you just read. Or you may write an essay on the person you interviewed, using direct quotes, paraphrases, and summaries of the interviewee's answers to your questions. Be sure to be accurate in reporting the interviewee's answers and ideas.

This excerpt is taken from Sheryl Luna's poetry collection, Pity the Drowned Horses, *published in 2005 by Notre Dame University Press. This collection won the Andres Montoya Poetry Prize. Luna is the 2008 recipient of the Alfredo Cisneros del Moral Foundation Award, and she currently teaches at the University of Colorado at Boulder.*

excerpt from

PITY THE DROWNED HORSES

BY SHERYL LUNA

I forgot how to speak. The old man with a gray
beard eyed me, waiting for Spanish.

Years of English rumbled something absent, forgotten.
The Tigua Indian Village, men at the corner bench eating
tamales. Indoors, tables with white formica,
floor-tiles peeling. In the steam of cilantro and tomato

Children sit cross-legged and sip caldo de res.
Men smoke afterward in faded jeans, and T-shirts lightly rise

around their pecs in the wind. It is how home is all
that's left in the end. The way we all return forever exiled.

History in mud houses and shady river-trees. Canal water
drifts. Children poke crawdads with dry branches. I spoke

Spanish broken, tongue-heavy. I was once too proud
to speak Spanish in the barrio. He waits for my voice.

His eyes generations. My brown skin a scandal on the hard streets
of El Paso. But, everyone loves a resurrection. Mauricio on a red

motor bike; Bob, a green-eyed white war hero, spits tobacco.
The sunlit desert and its gold light falling upon us. *Quiero*

aprender español, I whisper. He smiles. Blue hills
in the distance sharpen in an old elegance; the wind
hushes itself after howling the silences.

Which is your favorite image in the poem? Why? What does it say
to you?

What is Luna saying about language, specifically Spanish? What
significance does Spanish have for Luna? How do you know?

Select a classmate and interview them about their linguistic
background. How many languages and dialects do they speak? Which
is their "home" language? How do they feel about this language?
What are the uses for the other languages or dialects? Which one is
their favorite? Why? Which one is their strongest? Why? Do they
consider themselves monolingual, bilingual, or multilingual? Why?
Ask what their language(s) and dialect(s) say about their identity.

The following poem is taken from Gloria Anzaldúa's book Borderlands: La Frontera, *second edition published in 1999. This book is based on Anzaldúa's life growing up on the U.S.-México border. Anzaldúa, a leading scholar of Chicano cultural theory and Queer theory, received many awards, one being having* Borderlands: La Frontera *be recognized as one of the 100 Best Books of the Century by the* Utne Reader *and* The Hungry Mind Review. *As a Chicana feminist writer, Anzaldúa challenged the status quo of different cultural movements. She died in 2004, but her work continues to be recognized, cited, and used in academia.*

TO LIVE IN THE BORDERLANDS MEANS YOU

By Gloria Anzaldúa

To live in the Borderlands means you
    are neither *hispana india negra española*
     ni gabacha, eres estiza, mulata, half-breed caught in the
    crossfire between camps
    while carrying all five races on your back
    not knowing which side to turn to, run from;

To live in the Borderlands means
    knowing that the *india* in you, betrayed for 500 years,
    is no longer speaking to you,
    that *mexicanas* call you *rajetas,*
    that denying the Anglo inside you
    is as bad as having denied the Indian or Black;

Cuando vives en la frontera
    people walk through you, the wind steals your voice, you're a
        burra, buery, scapegoat,
    forerunner of a new race,
    half and half—both woman and man, neither—
    a new gender;

To live in the Borderlands means to
    put *chile* in the borscht,
    eat whole wheat *tortillas,*
    speak Tex-Mex with a Brooklyn accent;
    be stopped by *la migra* at the border checkpoints;

Living in the Borderlands means you fight hard to
    resist the gold elixir beckoning from the bottle,
    the pull of the gun barrel,
    the rope crushing the hollow of your throat;

In the Borderlands
 you are the battleground
 where enemies are kin to each other;
 you are at home, a stranger,
 the border disputes have been settled
 the volley of shots have shattered the truce
 you are wounded, lost in action
 dead, fighting back;

To live in the Borderlands means
 the mill with the razor white teeth wants to shred off
 your olive-red skin, crush out the kernel, your heart
 pound you pinch you roll you out
 smelling like white bread but dead;

To survive the Borderlands
 you must live *sin fronteras*
 be a crossroads.

---

gabacha—a Chicano term for a white woman
raletas—literally, "split," that is, having betrayed your word
burra—donkey
buey—oxen
sin fronteras—without borders

Explore

What is the message of Anzaldúa's poem? What examples from the poem suggest this?

Collaborate

In a small group, discuss what, according to Anzaldúa, it means to live in the Borderlands. How do you feel towards Anzaldúa as you read about her experience? Why do you feel this way?

Compose

Reflect on your own experiences as a human being. Have you ever felt as if you were at a crossroads? In an essay, describe such an experience from your life. This "crossroads" or "borderland" could involve nationality, ethnicity, gender, age, education, culture, language, or any other factor that contributes to your identity.

In the following debate, as U.S. border state governors, Arizona Governor Jan Brewer and New Mexico Governor Bill Richardson face off on immigration. Both governors present their positions and show different sides to immigration reform. This debate was published in the summer 2010 issue of the Americas Quarterly: The Policy Journal for Our Hemisphere.

HARD TALK: IMMIGRATION
JAN BREWER VS. BILL RICHARDSON

By Governors Jan Brewer & Bill Richardson

Should states and local governments have the right to enforce their own immigration laws when their voters decide the federal laws and practices are insufficient?

GOV. JAN BREWER

With the federal government unwilling to secure our border, we are left with little choice.

Our neighbor to the south is in a massive battle with well-organized drug cartels. Because of Washington's failure to secure our southern border, Arizona has become the superhighway for illegal drug and human smuggling activity. In December 2008, the U.S. Justice Department said that Mexican gangs are the "biggest organized crime threat to the United States." In 2009, Phoenix had 316 kidnapping cases, turning the city into our nation's kidnapping capital. Almost all of the persons kidnapped were undocumented immigrants or linked to the drug trade.

The same week that I signed the new law, a major drug ring was broken up and Mexican cartel operatives suspected of running 40,000 pounds of marijuana through southern Arizona were indicted.

While drug smuggling is the principal cause of our massive border violence problem, many of the same criminal organizations also smuggle people. Busts of drop houses, where undocumented immigrants are often held for ransom or otherwise severely abused, are not an uncommon occurrence in Arizona neighborhoods.

Today, Arizona has approximately 6,000 prison inmates who are foreign nationals, representing a cost to our state of roughly $150 million per year. Arizona taxpayers are paying for a vast majority of these incarceration expenses because the federal government refuses to pay what it owes. My predecessor as Arizona governor, current Homeland Security Secretary Janet Napolitano, sent numerous requests to the federal government to pay for these prisoners—only to be given the same answer that she and President Barack Obama are now giving Arizona: they will not pay the bill.

When I signed the legislation, I stated clearly I will not tolerate racial discrimination or racial profiling in Arizona. My administration worked for weeks with legislators to clarify and strengthen SB 1070's civil rights protections. I issued an executive order to implement proper training and enforcement protocols for our police so that the intent of the bill's language could not be misconstrued. Although it is already against the law, the new law undeniably prohibits law enforcement officers from considering race, color or national origin in implementing the new statute.

As committed as I am to protecting our state from crime associated with illegal immigration, I am equally committed to holding law enforcement accountable should this statute ever be misused to violate an individual's rights.

There have been countless distortions, honest omissions, myths, and bad information about Arizona's new law—many, undoubtedly, spread to create fear or mistrust.

So, here are the facts: first, the new Arizona law creates a state penalty to mirror what already is a federal crime. Despite the vile and hate-filled portrayals of proponents of the law as "Nazis"—actions that have been condemned nationally by the Anti-Defamation League—it is already a federal requirement for legal aliens in the U.S. to carry their green card or other immigration document. As anyone who has traveled abroad knows, other nations have similar laws.

Second, contrary to the horror stories being spread around (President Barack Obama, for example, suggested families risk being pulled over while going out for ice cream), law enforcement cannot randomly ask anyone about their immigration status. Much like the enforcement of seat belt laws in many states, under our new law there must first be reasonable suspicion that you are breaking some other non-immigration law before an officer can ask about your legal status. Only after another law has been broken can law enforcement officers inquire about immigration status if an individual's behavior provides "reasonable suspicion" that the person is here illegally. Reasonable suspicion is a well-understood concept that has been thoroughly vetted through numerous federal court cases. Racial profiling is prohibited in the new law. Examples of reasonable suspicion include a person running away when approached by law enforcement officers or a car failing to stop when the police turn on their lights.

Finally, Arizona's local law enforcement officers, who already reflect the great diversity of culture in our state, are going to be trained to enforce the new immigration law in a constitutional manner. It is shameful and presumptive for opponents to question the good will and the competence of Arizona's law enforcement personnel.

Theodore Roosevelt said, "No man is above the law and no man is below it; nor do we ask any man's permission when we require him to obey it. Obedience to the law is demanded as a right; not asked as a favor."

Arizona has been more than patient waiting for Washington to act. Decades of federal inaction and misguided policy have created a dangerous and unacceptable situation. Arizona has acted to enforce the rule of law, equally and without bias toward any person.

Polls show that a majority of Americans support Arizona's new law. As representatives elected by and for the people, we have an obligation to represent and protect our citizens to the best of our ability. The federal government has failed in its obligation and moral responsibility to secure our border. A government's principal responsibility to its citizens is to provide safety and security. States have never been expected, even in prosperous economic times, to sustain the national defense of our borders.

Arizona will no longer sit idly by and watch the destruction of our great state while the federal government watches from the sidelines. Although I recognize that SB 1070, as amended, is not the entire solution to our illegal immigration problem in Arizona, most people are united in the hope that it will finally inspire the politicians in Washington to stop talking and start acting now.

Janice K. Brewer *is the governor of Arizona.*

GOV. BILL RICHARDSON

U.S. national interest demands a uniform approach to immigration and foreign policy.

When the Arizona legislature decided to crack down on illegal immigration, it forced its state and local law enforcement agencies to enforce immigration law—or at least Arizona's version. But what if Arizona's new law drives more illegal immigration to the three remaining border states? How would those states react?

Imagine that legislators in California pass a law that denies business licenses to companies suspected of hiring undocumented immigrants. What if Texas sets up its own immigration inspections on state highways? And what would happen if New Mexico passes a law that closes the international ports of entry along the New Mexico–México border?

Sounds far-fetched, doesn't it? But it's easy to see how one state's actions related to a federal issue—immigration—could turn into the equivalent of an arms race among neighboring states.

The fact is, immigration and control of our international borders are federal issues for a reason. It is in America's national interest to have a uniform approach to an issue that affects foreign policy and national security.

That doesn't mean states should ignore the effects of illegal immigration or

The U.S. border fence near El Paso, TX

violence at the border. As governor, I have consistently taken state action to deal with the public safety of New Mexicans living near the border.

Ironically, while the Arizona bill may have been prompted by drug-related border violence, this law does nothing to solve the problem. In fact, the law may actually hurt law enforcement's ability to go after drug cartels because local police officers will be doing the work of the U.S. Border Patrol rather than the traditional crime fighting they are trained to do.

In 2005, I declared a state border emergency as a result of violence, damage to property and livestock, and increased drug smuggling near the New Mexico border town of Columbus. That emergency declaration freed up state money to pay for local law enforcement and a National Guard presence at the border to supplement the Border Patrol, which has primary responsibility for enforcement of federal immigration laws.

I also worked directly with my counterpart in the Mexican state of Chihuahua to address the border violence. Mexican authorities stepped up law enforcement in the area and agreed to bulldoze abandoned buildings across the border from Columbus that were used as staging areas to smuggle drugs and people.

We also worked with the governors of all Mexican border states through the Border Governors' Conference to address not just immigration and border violence but also education, health care and economic development in the region. We worked collectively as a group to get the attention of our respective federal governments, which is a much more productive way to address the need for immigration reform than enacting a hodge-podge of state laws—on either side of the border—that will only serve to exacerbate the problem.

Unfortunately, our federal government has not acted on our calls for comprehensive immigration reform, despite the public outcry. I am the first to acknowledge that this is a politically charged issue with no easy solutions. At the same time, I strongly disagree with Arizona's attempt to sidestep federal law and enforce immigration policy on its own.

We have to make immigration reform a national priority. We have to deal realistically with those undocumented workers who are already here. The reality is that we simply cannot deport everyone. Think about the costs that would entail: billions and billions of dollars spent on constant raids and round-ups that will only drive people further into the shadows. And by doing so, we will make them fearful of reporting crime. Immigrants will flee traffic accidents, no longer report domestic violence, and never report illegal operations by drug cartels.

My top priority when it comes to border security is the safety of New Mexico residents. I applaud President Felipe Calderón for his bold campaign against Mexican drug cartels. Unfortunately, the drug cartels are now waging their wars in and around border communities. I can't ignore the potential for that violence to spill over the border and into New Mexico. That is why I have funded additional law enforcement in those communities and recently sent National Guardsmen to once again support Border Patrol agents in the area.

We must work with México to address the root of the immigration problem. People are desperate to cross our borders because they are starved for hope. I believe that with strong national leadership we can get bipartisan support for a plan that does the following:

Secure the border by hiring and training enough Border Patrol agents to cover the entire border.

Establish a realistic path to legalization for those who are already here. This is not amnesty, but an effort that draws out those already here by offering legal status in exchange for good behavior, learning English, payment of back taxes, and fines for illegal entry.

Crack down on immigration fraud and undocumented workers.

Work in partnership with the Mexican government and other countries to develop border infrastructure and revitalize communities on both sides of the border to create much-needed jobs.

I understand the frustration that motivated Arizona's legislature to enact this new law. But this law is counter-productive and will further divide people. As the nation's only Hispanic governor, I am especially concerned about the likelihood for racial profiling in Arizona.

Nevertheless, I do not agree with those who advocate boycotts of Arizona as a result of this law. Like the law itself, boycotts are counter-productive and punish the people of Arizona.

Immigration is an issue that should remind us of what is great about America. But too often, it has brought out the worst in us, and the result has been a failure to reform the system. I know we can do better.

Bill Richardson *is the former governor of New Mexico.*

Research Arizona's new law, SB 1070. What does it state? What is Governor Brewer's position on this law? How does she dispute each of the arguments its opponents present?

In small groups, discuss the reasons Governor Richardson gives for why immigration and control of the U.S. international borders should be under federal jurisdiction and not the states'. What did Governor Richardson's declaration of a state border emergency in 2005 accomplish?

Hold a class debate. Half the class should support Governor Brewer's position, and the other half should support Governor Richardson's position. Clearly state each position. Offer specific reasons and support your arguments with valid evidence. Go to outside sources for support. Vote on which position was more persuasive and credible. What did the winning team do to win the debate?

BORDERS

The following document is taken from the manuscript "Myths about Immigration," in which Steven Mintz lists and describes the various myths surrounding immigration and its role in U.S. society. For the complete document go to http://www.truthinimmigration.org/Myths.aspx

MEXICAN AMERICAN LEGAL DEFENSE FUND, MYTHS ABOUT IMMIGRANTS, 2008

EXCERPT FROM TRUTHINIMMIGRATION.ORG
INTRODUCTION BY STEVEN MINTZ

In 1994, nearly 60 percent of California's voters approved Proposition 187, which would have prevented illegal immigrants from attending public schools and receiving social services and subsidized healthcare. The proposition would also have required law enforcement authorities, school administrators and social service and public health workers to turn in suspected illegal immigrants to federal and state authorities. Court rulings, however, prohibited implementation of the proposition and in July 1999, California decided not to appeal a federal court ruling that most provisions of the measure were unconstitutional. All that remains are laws that make it a crime to make or use false documents to conceal illegal immigrant status. (A 1982 Supreme Court decision, Plyer v. Doe, had guaranteed illegal immigrant children the right to a public education. One reason courts invalidated Proposition 187 is that immigration is regarded largely as a federal responsibility.)

During the mid-1990s, Proposition 187 was a national symbol of public anger about illegal immigration. It helped inspire Congress to include many bans on immigrant aid in the 1996 federal welfare overhaul. But the proposition increased political activity among Latinos and led a record number of immigrants to become citizens and register to vote.

Today, immigration to the United States is at its highest level since the early twentieth century. Some ten million legal and undocumented immigrants entered the country during the 1980s, exceeding the previous peak of nine million between 1900 and 1910.

As recently as the 1950s, two-thirds of all immigrants to the United States came from Europe or Canada. Today, more than 80 percent are Latin American or Asian. As a result of massive immigration, the United States is becoming the first truly multiracial advanced industrial society in which every resident will be a member of a minority group. California became the first state in which no single ethnic group or race makes up half of the population.

México has been the single largest contributor to American immigration. During the 1980s, the number of people of Mexican origin in the U.S. grew at five times the rate of the population as a whole. This surge was fueled by two factors: a high birth rate and the largest immigrant influx by any national group in American history. At least four million Mexicans immigrated to the United States in the 1980s—45 percent of the nine million immigrants who entered the country. Today, one out of every five immigrants now living in the US is Mexican born. Immigration was propelled by the rapid growth of México's population, which tripled in 50 years; by a financial, fiscal crisis in México; and by the wages to be found in the United States—at least six times higher than those in México. It also benefited from the unwillingness of the Mexican government to control immigration after the demise of the Bracero Program in 1964.

Work has been the great magnet pulling Mexican migrants to the United States. Historically, immigrants tackled menial jobs that native-born Americans avoided, such as digging canals, building railroads, or working in steel mills and garment factories. Today, the United States has a ravenous appetite for service workers, non-unionized manufacturing workers, farm workers, and skilled artisans. Mexican workers have met those needs. Fear of detection and expulsion keeps many immigrant workers from taking advantage of social welfare programs and makes them highly vulnerable to exploitation by employers.

Each wave of immigrants has also sparked a wave of anti-immigrant sentiment. Since the first wave of mass immigration from Germany and Ireland in the 1840s, nativists have expressed fear that immigrants depress wages, displace workers, and threaten the nation's cultural values and security. Although Americans celebrate the United States as a melting pot of cultures and nationalities, they have not been eager to embrace immigrants who prefer not to surrender their native identity, language, or traditions. The most recent upsurge in nativism arose during the economic recession of the early and mid-1990s, when California's voters passed Proposition 187.

Nineteenth-century nativists charged Catholic immigrants with being subservient to a foreign leader, the Pope; later xenophobes accused immigrants of carrying subversive ideologies. Today's critics are more concerned about immigration's economic costs and the erosion of what they see as the nation's traditional culture. Many fear that newcomers made use of services like welfare or unemployment benefits more frequently than natives. Some argue that the new wave of immigrants is less skilled than its predecessors and is therefore more likely to become a burden on the government. There are concerns that US society is being split into separate and unequal societies divided by skin color, ethnic background, language, and culture. Belief that immigrants are attracted to the United States by welfare benefits led Congress in 1996 to restrict the access of non-citizens to social services.

Yet others welcome the increasing population diversity, cherishing the extraordinary variety of their country's people.

MYTH: America has "uncontrolled" and "unprecedented" immigration.

While the immigrant population is the highest it's ever been in absolute numbers, it isn't so when compared to the equally increasing total U.S. population. Since the beginning of the 20th century, the percentage of immigrants has fluctuated within 5-15% of the U.S. population. As of 2006, immigrants are 12% of the U.S. population.

© Todd Bigelow

MYTH: Most undocumented immigrants are Mexican adult males illegally crossing the border.

There were between 11.5 and 12 million unauthorized immigrants in 2006. The calculations reported suggest that roughly 4.5 to 6 million (or 40 to 50% of the total) entered the country legally through ports of entry.

About 56 percent of the unauthorized population was from México, and another 22 percent from elsewhere in Latin America. The rest come from

Muddy footprints across a highway show the path undocumented migrants took entering the country from Agua Prieta, México into Douglas, Arizona

Asia, Europe, Canada, Africa, and elsewhere (Immigration Policy Center, Spring 2007).

MYTH: Today's immigrants are different than those 100 years ago: they "refuse" to assimilate.

According to a recent United Way of Salt Lake survey, more than 80 percent of immigrants and refugees say they have formally tried to learn English. Many more say they've tried by speaking English to friends or by listening to English-language radio and television.

Learning a second language can be difficult for any adult, but top barriers to English acquisition for immigrants (who often work two or three separate jobs) include lack of time, lack of childcare, and difficulty of task.

All social science data points to the fact that immigrants are assimilating as fast as previous generations of immigrants. While immigrant parents may struggle with learning a new language, 91% of second-generation Hispanics can speak English well, as can 97% of third-generation Hispanics.

MYTH: Immigrants are violent criminals "overflowing" our prisons.

In 2000, three percent of the 45.2 million males age 18 to 39 in the United States were in federal or state or local jails at the time of the census. The incarceration rate of native-born men in this age group was five times higher than the incarceration rate of foreign-born men.

Among the U.S.-born, 9.8 percent of all male high school dropouts were in jail or prison in 2000. Only 1.3 percent of immigrant men who were high school dropouts were incarcerated.

MYTH: Immigrants are a financial burden on taxpayers.

While the myth that undocumented immigrants are an economic drain is widespread, "every empirical study of illegal's economic impact demonstrates the opposite...; undocumented actually contribute more to public coffers in taxes than they cost in social services."

Undocumented immigrants are ineligible for most federally funded benefits including cash assistance, food stamps, and SSI.

A study by economists Richard Vedeer, Lowell Gallaway, and Stephen Moore found that states with relatively high immigration actually experience low unemployment. The economists believed that it is likely immigration opens up many job opportunities for natives.

Explore

Research both Proposition 187 and the 1982 Supreme Court decision, Plyer vs. Doe. What is each proposing? Why was one rejected and the other implemented?

Invent

Create your own list of myths on immigration. For example, many believe the myth that more immigrants mean more crime in the country. State each one of your myths clearly and explain why it is a myth.

Compose

Select one of the myths listed by Mintz. Write an argumentative essay in which you either support the myth as being just a myth, or disagree with Mintz and argue why it is not a myth, but a fact. Research your position. Support it with valid evidence, examples, and sources.

A native El Pasoan, Mario T. Garcia has written many books on Chicano history. Several of these have been awarded prizes, including the Southwest Book Award. Currently, Garcia teaches at the University of California, Santa Barbara and is the director of the Latino Leadership Project at the university's Chicano Studies Institute.

INTRODUCTION TO RUBEN SALAZAR: BORDER CORRESPONDENT

By Mario T. Garcia

On August 29, 1970, in East Los Angeles, Chicanos staged the largest antiwar demonstration ever organized in the United States by people of Mexican descent. More than twenty thousand marched in a spirited Chicano moratorium against the Vietnam War. Demonstrators came from all over southern California as well as from other parts of the state and from the Southwest. Although predominantly young, the demonstrators included older Mexican Americans. They protested, like Americans across the country, a war that many of them had initially supported. After years of seeing their young men killing and being killed, Chicanos began to question the reasons for the bloodshed and the U.S. role in the conflict. It was an especially relevant issue for Chicanos since they, like African Americans, were being drafted in numbers disproportionate to their percentage of the total population. And once in the military, they were again being killed in numbers disproportionate to their representation in the armed forces.[1] Hundreds of Chicanos were returning in body bags or seriously maimed, both physically and psychologically. For young Chicanos now further engaged at home in a militant social movement for self-determination and self-identity—the Chicano movement—the Vietnam War represented one more example of the ongoing exploitation of Mexicans in the United States, beginning with the U.S. seizure of half of México's territory—virtually the entire Southwest—in the mid-nineteenth century.

And so they marched and protested that fateful day in August, down Brooklyn and Whittier avenues until they converged on Laguna Park. They arrived by the thousands and were greeted with Mexican music and a festive atmosphere on a filtered sunny/smoggy L.A. day. As the first to arrive sat on the grass, watching the rest of the marchers streaming in, they listened to the entertainment and to the speakers. But apprehension soon began to set in among the crowd, and then intermittent police sirens were heard. Rumors began to spread about a disturbance on Whittier Boulevard: police were roughing up and arresting some of the demonstrators. As the crowd turned to look, they saw the ominous arrival of hundreds of helmeted police—Los Angeles County Sheriff's deputies—who were assembling at one end of the park, some wearing gas masks. Without warning (the Sheriff's Department would later claim provocation on the part of the demonstrators) they moved on the crowd. Pandemonium broke out as the deputies fired tear gas canisters into the dispersing assembly of men, women, and children. Some of the Chicanos fought back. They pelted the deputies with their own tear gas canisters and whatever else they could find. The deputies charged into the crowd. Flaying nightsticks found their marks. A young Chicana was struck on the back of her head and fell to the ground. Tears from the gas mingled with blood and streamed down the faces of the demonstrators. Moratorium leaflets were dropped and scattered on the streets.[2]

Out of the park, many Chicanos began to vent their anger and frustration at having their peaceful moratorium violently repressed by the police—another example of the oppression of La Raza. Windows were broken, cars were set on fire, and rocks were thrown. Reinforcement deputies arrived and joined in the beatings. That afternoon, East L.A. became a battleground.[3]

Ruben Salazar, a columnist for the *Los Angeles Times* and the news director of KMEX, the Spanish-language TV station in Los Angeles, covered the moratorium that day. He and his TV crew witnessed much of the disturbance. Later that afternoon, they retired to the Silver Dollar Café on Whittier Boulevard to relax and have a beer. According to the cameraman, Guillermo Restrepo, Salazar believed that he and his crew were being followed after the breakup of the moratorium.[4] Shortly after arriving, they heard a police radio outside the café. Through the window they saw armed deputies in riot gear. The deputies ordered everyone outside back into the café, and without warning, a tear gas projectile blasted through the door. Another canister—a ten-inch missile—smashed into the café. Two others followed. The deputies would later claim that they had been told that an armed individual was inside the café, but no weapon ever turned up. Behind the café, Salazar's colleagues realized that Salazar was still inside. Their attempts to go back and find him were rebuffed by the deputies. Despite his friends' insistence that Salazar remained in the café, the deputies refused to check inside or allow anyone to enter. When the deputies finally entered several hours later, Salazar's body was found. One of the projectiles, an inquest later determined, had torn through his head.[5]

Raul Ruiz and Joe Razo of *La Raza* magazine, a Chicano movement publication, happened to find themselves across from the Silver Dollar at the time. At the first signs of a disturbance, both began to photograph the actions of the Sheriff's deputies. Their photographs, later published in both *La Raza* and the *Los Angeles Times*, revealed that one of the deputies fired directly into the café. Ruben Salazar was forty-two at the time of his death. He left a wife and three children.[6]

Two other people died at the moratorium, and sixty-one were injured. More than two hundred were arrested, and property damage reached over $1 million.[7] When the news of Salazar's death reached the Chicano community, its anger and hatred toward the police were mixed with great sorrow over the death of a journalist whom many in the community knew and respected. The inquest into his death was televised and lasted sixteen days. According to the Los Angeles County Coroner Thomas T. Noguchi, whose office conducted an autopsy of Salazar's body, Salazar had died almost instantly from a "through-and-through projectile wound of the left temple area causing massive injury to the brain."[8]

The police, including Deputy Thomas Wilson, who fired the missile, were questioned, as were some of the Chicanos who were at the moratorium. One of the key issues was whether Wilson was acting in accordance with proper procedures when he fired the projectiles. This question, however, was never examined because the Sheriff's Department refused to turn over its training manual, which covered the use of tear gas equipment, and the manual was never subpoenaed by the inquest officer, Norman Pittluck. According to Sheriff Peter Pitchess, "There was absolutely no misconduct on the part of the deputies involved or in the procedures they followed."[9]

Instead the questioning turned into an indictment of the moratorium. The District Attorney's office, which was supposed to remain neutral so as to determine the facts of the case, in fact functioned as defense attorneys for the Sheriff's Department. The moratorium, it was suggested by Pittluck, was an unruly mob determined to do violence. And the Sheriff's deputies, furthermore, were there only to protect the community and restore law and order. The demonstrators were also portrayed as subversives: "Is that Castro's man?" Raul Ruiz was asked about a photograph that showed some of the demonstrators holding a picture of Che Guevara. "Che Guevara," Ruiz responded, "was a great hero to the people of Latin America. He struggled against oppression and injustice." The Chicanos in the court cheered, and the jury ruled by a 4 to 3 vote that Salazar had met death "at the hands of another."[10]

Che Guevara

However, District Attorney, Evelle Younger, concluded that the facts from the inquest did not justify criminal charges against Deputy Wilson or the Sheriff's Department. According to Younger, no criminal intent on the part of Wilson or the other Sheriff's deputies could be determined. Younger further concluded that the split decision by the jury suggested that it would be difficult to convince a trial jury that a crime had been committed. The Department of Justice added insult to injury when it also refused to investigate Salazar's death after requested to do so by twenty-two California state legislators.[11]

The case was closed for the police and the investigating officials but not for Chicanos, who held the police guilty of murder. A well-known Chicano attorney and subsequent celebrity, Oscar Zeta Acosta—aka the "Brown Buffalo"—accused authorities of criminal conspiracy to commit political assassination, another vicious example of police state tactics in America with precedents not confined to the Chicano community.[12] Acosta was twice forcibly ejected from the hearing room for protesting the injustice of the hearing. The ejections in turn provoked scuffles in the courtroom between Chicanos and courtroom deputies.[13] Danny Villanueva, who was then station manager of KMEX and Salazar's boss, is perplexed to this day by the lack of prosecution of the officers involved in the Silver Dollar incident. "If there wasn't a conspiracy," he concludes, "it is an incredible set of circumstances."[14]

The protests continued, and the Chicano movement had another martyr. Yet, ironically, and despite the many dangerous assignments he undertook throughout his career, Salazar would never have conceived of himself in this way. Salazar was neither a martyr nor a politico but a hardworking reporter whose career and work needs to be appreciated beyond his tragic death.

Salazar can be seen as a "border correspondent," not only because he himself was literally a product of the U.S.-Mexican border or because he covered the U.S.-Mexican border as a reporter at one point in his career but symbolically as well. Salazar's career was marked by crossing new borders or frontiers. Although there exists a long history of Mexican American journalism in the United States, primarily catering to a Mexican American or *mexicano* immigrant population, Salazar was the first journalist of Mexican American background to cross over into mainstream English-language journalism.[15] He was the first Mexican American journalist to work as a reporter for the *Los Angeles Times*. He was the first Mexican American journalist to become an important foreign correspondent. And he was the first Mexican American journalist to have a column in a major American English-language newspaper.

In his short career, ended too soon, Salazar crossed a variety of borders, certainly professional ones and undoubtedly personal ones as well. This work is dedicated to examining Salazar as a professional border crosser—a border correspondent.

WHO WAS RUBEN SALAZAR?

While little is known about Salazar's early life, we do know some general facts. He was born on March 3, 1928 in Ciudad Juárez—"Juaritos," as the Chicanos on the other side of the border in El Paso called this notorious Mexican border town. When Ruben was eight months old his parents moved across the shallow Rio Grande and settled in El Paso, or "El Chuco," as it was known by the Chicanos and pachucos of the 1940s and 1950s. There Ruben became a naturalized citizen. His father worked at a downtown jewelry store, where he was in charge of the silver department. This job paid well, apparently the Salazar family enjoyed a middle-class life in El Paso. After graduating from El Paso High School, Salazar served in the U.S. Army in Germany from 1950 to 1952. In the early fifties, as a result of his own ambition and the encouragement of his parents, Salazar became one of the few Mexican Americans to attend college. He chose Texas Western College, later to become the University of

Texas at El Paso, where he majored in journalism and wrote a few pieces for *El Burro*, the campus paper. After graduation, he joined the *El Paso Herald-Post*, the first Mexican American reporter for that paper. The editor, Ed Pooley, had been a longtime champion of Mexican Americans, who, because they lacked education and a political voice (even though they represented the majority in El Paso) had few employment opportunities and most often lived in poverty.[16]

CUB REPORTER

Salazar's work during his apprenticeship at the *El Paso Herald-Post* is obscured by the lack of byline articles carrying his name. Nevertheless, according to Earl Shorris, who began his career at the *Herald-Post* while Salazar was there, Pooley thought Salazar could do no wrong and considered him to be his best reporter.[17] What can be identified as Salazar's own work confirms his talent as a reporter and provides some fascinating reading, especially a short series of investigative pieces. Assigned to the police and Juárez beats and aware of the poverty and accompanying alienation of many Chicanos in this border city, Salazar volunteered to investigate the Chicano underworld. For one story, "25 Hours in Jail—I Lived in a Chamber of Horrors" (May 9, 1955), Salazar had himself booked on a phony drunk charge in order to experience conditions in the city jail. He was locked in Tank 6 along with several other Chicanos. Salazar reported on the filthy and repulsive conditions of the jail, where the prisoners had easy access to drugs. Under the influence of drugs and alcohol and almost totally unsupervised, the inmates committed violent acts against each other. After one night, Salazar had had enough. "I left the jail," he wrote, "knowing how it feels to live in a hophead Chamber of Horrors."

Shorris recalls that Arturo Islas, who was on the detective staff of the El Paso Police Department, remarked after the story broke that he had seen Salazar in jail but assumed that Salazar had indeed been arrested for being drunk and therefore had done nothing to secure his release. Shorris further notes that the jail story quickly became the journalistic coup of the decade in El Paso. Before that story the local newspapers had carried very little investigative reporting. According to Shorris, Salazar's story and similar pieces helped change the nature of journalism in El Paso.[18]

In another investigative story (August 17, 1955), on La Nacha, the dope queen of the border, Salazar posed as a drug user. He hired a drug addict known as "Hypo" for $15 to demonstrate a purchase from La Nacha. Accompanying

Hypo, Salazar visited La Nacha's home in the barrio and revealed to his readers how easy and open the trade in drugs, including heroin, was in El Paso.

It was just as easy for poor down-and-outs to purchase homemade liquor from one of the several speakeasies in South El Paso, the main barrio. On this story (July 3, 1956), Salazar met Chencha, the queen of the speakeasies, who was famous for her ten-cent shot of the potentially lethal "alky." "It rasped my throat like sandpaper," Salazar wrote. While these early Salazar pieces contain some stereotyping of Chicanos, they are also poignant expressions of the plight of the inhabitants of this Chicano underworld. They achieve an intense social realism, a kind of muckraking social reformism, and they reveal Salazar's willingness to investigate a story even under the most difficult conditions. According to Shorris, these stories made Salazar into something of a hero in El Paso. "Ruben was the best reporter El Paso had ever seen," Shorris concludes.[19]

Like many of the other reporters at the *Herald-Post*, Salazar, according to Shorris, possessed the ambition and the dream of eventually moving on to California, specifically, to the Los Angeles papers.[20] Consequently, sometime in 1956 or 1957, Salazar moved to California, where he first worked for the *Santa Rosa Press Democrat* and a short time later moved on to the *San Francisco News*. After moving to southern California in the late 1950s, Salazar found a position with the *Los Angeles Herald-Express*. In 1959 Salazar got his big break and joined the *Los Angeles Times*. It was with the *Times* that Salazar would mature as a journalist.[21]

NOTES

1. See Ralph Guzmán, "Mexican American Casualties in Vietnam," *La Raza* (1970), Vol. I, no. 1, 12-15.

2. On the Chicano moratorium, see special issue of *La Raza* (1970), Vol. I, no. 3. Also see Rodolfo Acuña, *Occupied America: A History of Chicanos*, 3d ed. (New York: Harper-Collins, 1988), 345-350; Oscar Zeta Acosta, *The Revolt of the Cockroach People* (New York: Bantam, 1974; orig. pub. 1973); and the film documentary Requiem 29 (1970; produced by Moctesuma Esparza and directed by David García).

3. Ibid.

4. Interview with Danny Villanueva, February 8, 1994, by Mario T. Garcia. Also see Edward J. Escobar, "The Dialectics of Repression: The Los Angeles Police Department and the Chicano Movement, 1968-1971," *Journal of American History 79*, no. 4 (March 1993): p. 1503.

5. See *La Raza* (1970), Vol. I, no. 3 and Acuña, *Occupied America*, 345-350.

6. Ibid; Raul Ruíz, "August 29th & the Death of Ruben Salazar," in program for production of "August 29" produced by the Los Angeles Theatre Center Latino Theatre Lab and directed by José Valenzuela in 1990 on the 20th anniversary of Salazar's death.

7. Ibid.

8. See José Angel de La Vera, "1970 Chicano Moratorium and Death of Ruben Salazar," in Manuel P. Servin, ed., *An Awakened Minority: Mexican-Americans* (Beverly Hills: Glencoe Press, 1974), 274.

9. Ibid, 281

10. See *Requiem 29*; de La Vera, "Chicano Moratorium."

11. See de la Vera, "Chicano Moratorium," 279, 281.

12. See Acosta, *Cockroach People*. For transcripts of the Salazar inquest, see Oscar Zeta Acosta collection in the California Ethnic and Multicultural Archives (CEMA) in Special Collections at the University of California, Santa Barbara, Library.

13. See de La Vera, "Chicano Moratorium," 278.

14. Villanueva Interview.

15. Examples of such nineteenth-and twentieth-century newspapers exist in microfilm. These include *La Prensa* (San Antonio) and *La Opinión* (Los Angeles). Also see my chapter on the Mexican-American journalist Ignacio López publisher of *El Espectator* in the Pomona Valley of southern California from the 1930s through the 1950s, "Mexican-American Muckraker: Ignacio L. López and *El Espectator*" in Mario T. García, *Mexican Americans: Leadership, Ideology, and Identity, 1930-1960* (New Haven: Yale University Press, 1989), 84-112.

16. See Ruben Salazar résumé in Ruben Salazar File with the *Los Angeles Times*. Interview with Earl Shorris, February 28, 1994 by Mario T. García. On Pooley and the *El Paso Herald-Post*, see García, *Mexican Americans*, 113-141.

17. Shorris interview.

18. Ibid.

19. Ibid.

20. Ibid

21. Salazar résumé.

Explore

What is the Chicano Movement? Who is a Chicano?

Collaborate

With a classmate, go online and search for *La Raza* magazine. Examine the different issues addressed in this periodical. How would you describe the content? What issues are addressed? What is the magazine's purpose and intended audience?

Compose

Write a profile of either Ruben Salazar or Che Guevara. If writing about Guevara, consider the following questions: Who is Che Guevara? What role did he play in the Chicano movement? Why is he important to the people of Latin America? If writing about Salazar, consider the following question: What "borders" did Salazar cross?

BORDERS

Born in Juárez, México and raised in El Paso, TX, Ruben Salazar was a journalist and a reporter at the El Paso Herald-Post. Among his accomplishments are: being the first Mexican American reporter to work at an El Paso newspaper, the first Mexican American columnist at the Los Angeles Times, and the first Mexican American foreign correspondent in the U.S. intervention in the Dominican Republic. After his death, Salazar was awarded a Robert F. Kennedy Award, was honored with the issuance of a first class stamp in 2008, and was honored by his alma mater, the University of Texas at El Paso with the creation of the Ruben Salazar Spanish Language Media Program in 2003.

MILITANTS FIGHT TO RETAIN SPANISH AS THEIR LANGUAGE

By Ruben Salazar

EL PASO – The SPANISH LANGUAGE, SPOKEN in the Southwest long before Plymouth Bay and Jamestown were settled, is under fire in some quarters as being detrimental to Americanism.

The result is that militant Mexican-Americans, who prefer to call themselves Chicanos, are fighting back with a rising chauvinism which had begun to blur after years of conditioning by U.S. society.

Throughout the Southwest, and especially along the Mexican border, the old controversy of whether Mexican-American students should speak Spanish in school and on the playground is stirring racial sensitivities.

In the lower Rio Grande Valley, more than half of 150 high school students demonstrating against a rule that prohibited the use of Spanish on the playground were recently arrested.

STUDENTS THREATEN WALKOUT

In El Paso, students threatened a massive walkout at Bowie High School, composed of about 95% Mexican-Americans, over a rule against students speaking Spanish. The rule was enforced with detention for any violations.

In both cases the defenders won the day—the lower Rio Grande Valley students were exonerated and the contested rule at Bowie was rescinded. Nevertheless, the issue, long an explosive one in the Southwest, is again out in the open with its complicated implications.

Shortly after the Rio Grande Valley and the El Paso incidents, Mexican-American high school students at Uvalde—the Texas hometown of the late Vice President John N. Garner*—staged a "Chicano happening."

Attending the year-end school dance, which is the semester's big affair, Mexican-American students showed up in Mexican ponchos, while the rest of the students came dressed in conventional dark suits and long dresses. The Mexican-Americans then segregated themselves from the rest of the crowd and started making tacos with tortillas, chili and meat which the girls had brought in containers.

It caused a stir, not only among Anglo students, parents and teachers, but also among Mexican-American parents who couldn't understand why their children were "disgracing" themselves after they (the parents) had worked so hard to give them clothes like the ones the other students wore.

PUZZLED BY YOUTH

Mike Gonzales, an attorney and controversial Mexican-American leader in Del Rio, said: "Anglos and older Mexican-Americans just don't seem to know what is happening. Mexican-American kids are in the throes of self-identification."

Use of the Spanish language, say other leaders, is one thing that Mexican-Americans have over other students and they tend to exploit it.

The controversy centers on two arguments:

Mexican-American students should concentrate on English because speaking Spanish too much hurts their proficiency in the "national language," English. Besides, said a school psychologist, children growing up in a bicultural environment are more prone than others to neurosis and mental disorders.

Mexicans are indigenous to the Southwest, and so the Spanish language is part of their culture which should not be tampered with. Having colonized the Southwest, Spanish-speaking people refuse to abandon their traditions because of the advent of Anglo-American culture.

The controversy is not one of whether Spanish, or any other foreign language, should be taught in school. All educators agree that a person is better off speaking two or more languages. But some school officials object to Mexican-American students speaking Spanish in school and on the playground not only on the basis of it being detrimental to their English but because it irks other students who don't speak Spanish.

In south Texas, a teacher, commenting on the controversial issue, wrote a pamphlet which reads in part:

"They are good people. Their only handicap is the bag full of superstitions and silly notions they inherited from México. When they get rid of these superstitions, they will be good Americans. Their schools help more than anything else."

CHANGE FORESEEN

"In time, the Latin will think and act like Americans. A lot depends on whether we can get them to switch from Spanish to English. When they speak English at home like the rest of us, they will be part of the American way of life. I just don't understand why they are so insistent about using Spanish. They should realize that it's not the American tongue."

This approach infuriates the growing number of militant Mexican-American leaders, many of whom now insist that meetings held to discuss the problems of this ethnic group should be conducted in Spanish.

Some education experts say that what is needed in the Southwest is for non-Mexican-Americans to become "Mexicanized"—not the other way around. Asked how the Mexican-American can find his way into U.S. Society, Dr. Jack D. Forbes, research program director of UC Berkeley's Far West Laboratory for Educational Research and Development, recently told the U.S. Civil Rights Commission:

"The Anglo-American, quite obviously, is the new-comer." It is the Anglo-American, he said, who should learn more about the Mexican-American, his heritage and his culture. No one, he continued, can truly call himself a Southwesterner "unless he is a Mexicanized person to a considerable degree."

NOT ENOUGH

To the extremist Mexican-American leaders not even this is enough. What these leaders want for the 5 million Mexican-Americans in the five Southwestern states—California, Arizona, Colorado, New Mexico, Texas—is separatism not a "Mexicanized" society.

The controversial New Mexico Spanish-speaking leader, Reies Lopez Tijerina, who preaches to his followers that they should speak Spanish as often as possible, is a prime advocate of a separate—but equal—state for Mexican-Americans.**

Though few take the separatist movement seriously, educators in the Southwest worry about Mexican-Americans retreating into a "Mexican shell." Not only are many Mexican-American students affecting Mexican rural dress but many have posters in their bedrooms depicting such Mexican revolutionary heroes as Emiliano Zapata and slogans reading "Primero la Raza" (the Mexican race first).

"Attempts to prohibit the use of the Spanish language, no matter how lofty the reasons, will only make things worse," says an El Paso teacher.

Those who would try to abolish the use of Spanish in informal situations in school and on the playground are guilty of the "cowboy-and-Indian viewpoint," says Harold Howe II, former U.S. Commissioner Education.

*John Nance Garner served as vice president of the United States between 1933 and 1936 under Franklin Delano Roosevelt.

** Beginning in 1963, Reies Lopez Tijerina organized the Alianza Federal de Mercedes in New Mexico to renew claims to land grants stolen from Mexican Americans as a result of the conquest and annexation of New Mexico by the United States in 1848.

Create two lists: One listing the reasons why the Bowie High School walkout was an effective course of action by the students, and the other listing reasons why the walkout was a bad idea.

Write an essay in which you take a position on language in schools. Should only English be spoken in U.S. schools? Should students' home languages be allowed in the classroom? Why? Why not? When? For what purpose(s)? Support your position and reasons with evidence of your choice.

The following excerpt is from Americo Paredes's Folklore and Culture on the Texas-Mexican Border, published in 1993. Paredes is Dickson, Allen, and Anderson Centennial Professor Emeritus of Anthropology and English at the University of Texas at Austin, where he has taught folklore since 1957. He received the Charles Frankel Prize in 1989, and in 1990, México's government awarded Paredes La Orden Mexicana del Aguila Azteca, the highest award bestowed to citizens of other countries.

THE PROBLEMS OF IDENTITY IN A CHANGING CULTURE: POPULAR EXPRESSIONS OF CULTURE CONFLICT ALONG THE LOWER RIO GRANDE BORDER

BY AMÉRICO PAREDES

. . . Friends and relatives who had been near neighbors—within shouting distance across a few hundred feet of water—now were legally in different countries. If they wanted to visit each other, the law required that they travel many miles up- or downstream, to the nearest official crossing place, instead of swimming or boating directly across as they used to do before. . .

-Américo Paredes

Conflict—cultural, economic, and physical—has been a way of life along the border between México and the United States, and it is in the so-called Nueces-Rio Grande strip where its patterns were first established. Problems of identity also are common to border dwellers, and these problems were first confronted by people of Mexican culture as a result of the Texas Revolution. For these reasons, the lower Rio Grande area also can claim to be the source of the more typical elements of what we call the culture of the border.

Life along the border was not always a matter of conflicting cultures; there was often cooperation of a sort, between ordinary people of both cultures, since life had to be lived as an everyday affair. People most often cooperated in circumventing the excessive regulation of ordinary intercourse across the border. In other words, they regularly were engaged in smuggling.

Borders offer special conditions not only for smuggling but for the idealization of the smuggler. This sounds pretty obvious since, after all, political boundaries are the obvious places where customs and immigration regulations are enforced. But we must consider not only the existence of such political boundaries but the circumstances of their creation. In this respect, the lower Rio Grande border was especially suited for smuggling operations.

To appreciate this fact, one has only to consider that when the Treaty of Guadalupe Hidalgo officially settled the conflict over territory between México and the United States, a very well defined geographic feature, the Rio Grande itself, became the international line. But it was a line that cut right through the middle of what had once been the Mexican province of Nuevo Santander. Friends and relatives who had been near neighbors—within shouting distance across a few hundred feet of water—now were legally in different countries. If they wanted to visit each other, the law required that they travel many miles up- or downstream, to the nearest official crossing place, instead of swimming or boating directly across as they used to do before. It goes without saying that they paid little attention to the requirements of the law. When they went visiting, they crossed at the most convenient spot on the river; and, as is ancient custom when one goes visiting loved ones, they took gifts with them: farm products from México to Texas, textiles and other manufactured goods from Texas to México. Legally, of course, this was smuggling, differing from contraband for profit in volume only. Such a pattern is familiar to anyone who knows the border, for it still operates, not only along the lower Rio Grande now but all along the boundary line between México and the United States.

Unofficial crossings also disregarded immigration laws. Children born on one side of the river would be baptized on the other side, and thus appear on church registers as citizens of the other country. This bothered no one since people on both sides of the river thought of themselves as mexicanos, but U.S. officials were concerned about it. People would come across to visit relatives and stay long periods of time, and perhaps move inland in search of work. After 1890, the movement in search of work was preponderantly from México deep into Texas and beyond. The ease with which the river could be crossed and the hospitality of relatives and friends on either side also was a boon to men who got in trouble with the law. It was not necessary to flee over trackless wastes, with the law hot on one's trail. All it took was a few moments in the water, and one was out of reach of his pursuers and in the hands of friends. If illegal crossings in search of work were mainly in a northerly direction, crossings to escape the law were for the most part from north to south. By far, not all the Mexicans fleeing American law were criminals in an ordinary sense. Many were victims of cultural conflict, men who had reacted violently to assaults on their human dignity or their economic rights.

Resulting from the partition of the lower Rio Grande communities was a set of folk attitudes that would in time become general along the U.S.-Mexican border. There was a generally favorable disposition toward the individual who disregarded customs and immigration laws, especially the laws of the United States. The professional smuggler was not a figure of reproach, whether he was engaged in smuggling American woven goods into México or Mexican tequila into Texas. In folklore there was a tendency to idealize the smuggler, especially the tequilero, as a variant of the hero of cultural conflict. The smuggler, the illegal alien looking for work, and the border-conflict hero became identified with each other in the popular mind. They came

National Migration Week 2011 Drawing

into conflict with the same American laws and sometimes with the same individual officers of the law, who were all looked upon as rinches-- a border-Spanish rendering of "ranger." Men who were Texas rangers, for example, during the revenge killings of Mexicans after the Pizana uprising of 1915[1] later were border patrolmen who engaged in gun battles with tequileros. So stereotyped did the figure of the rinche become that lower Rio Grande border versions of "La Persecucion de Villa" identify Pershing's soldiers as rinches.

A "corrido" (ballad) tradition of intercultural conflict developed along the Rio Grande, in which the hero defends his rights and those of other Mexicans against the rinches. The first hero of these corridos is Juan Nepomuceno Cortina, who is celebrated in an 1859 corrido precisely because he helps a fellow Mexican.

Other major corrido heroes are Gregorio Cortez (1901), who kills two Texas sheriffs after one of them shoots his brother; Jacinto Trevino (1911), who kills several Americans to avenge his brother's death; Rito Garcia (1885), who shoots several officers who invade his home without a warrant; and Aniceto Pizana and his "sediciosos" (1915). Some corrido heroes escape across the border into México; others, like Gregorio Cortez and Rito Garcia, are betrayed and captured. They go to prison but they have stood up for what is right. As the "Corrido de Rito Garcia" says,

> . . . me voy a la penitencia
> por defender mi derecho.

> . . . I am going to the penitentiary
> because l defended my rights.

The men who smuggled tequila into the United States during the 20s and early 30s were no apostles of civil rights, nor did the border people think of them as such. But in his activities, the tequilero risked his life against the old enemy, the rinche. And, as has been noted, smuggling had long been part of the border way of life. Still sung today is "EI Corrido de Mariano Resendez," about a prominent smuggler of textiles into México, circa 1900. So highly respected were Resendez and his activities that he was known as "EI Contrabandista." Resendez, of course, violated Mexican laws, and his battles were with Mexican customs officers. The tequilero and his activities, however, took on an intercultural dimension and became a kind of coda to the corridos of border conflict.

The heavy-handed and often brutal manner that Anglo lawmen have used in their dealings with border Mexicans helped make almost any man outside the law a sympathetic figure, with the rinche, or Texas ranger, as the symbol of police brutality. That these symbols still are alive may be seen in the recent Fred Carrasco affair. The border Mexican's tolerance of smuggling does not seem to extend to traffic in drugs. The few corridos that have been current on the subject, such as "Carga blanca," take a negative view of the dope peddler. Yet Carrasco's death in 1976 at the Huntsville, Texas, prison along with two women hostages inspired close to a dozen corridos with echoes of the old style. The sensational character of Carrasco's death cannot be discounted, but note should also be taken of the unproved though widely circulated charges that Carrasco was "executed" by a Texas ranger, who allegedly shot him through the head at close range where Carrasco lay wounded. This is a scenario familiar to many a piece of folk literature about cultural conflict—corridos and prose narratives—the rinche finishing off the wounded Mexican with a bullet through the head. It is interesting to compare the following stanzas, the first from one of the Carrasco corridos and the other two from a tequilero ballad of the '30s.

> El capitan de los rinches
> fue el primero que cayo
> pero el chaleco de malla
> las balas no traspaso.

> The captain of the rangers
> was the first one to fall,
> but the armored vest he was wearing
> did not let the bullets through.

> En fin de tanto invitarle
> Leandro los acompano;
> en las lomas de Almiramba
> fue el primero que cayo.

> They kept asking him to go,
> until Leandro went with them;
> in the hills of Almiramba
> he was the first one to fall.

> El capitan de los rinches
> a Silvano se acerco
> y en unos cuantos segundos
> Silvano Garcia murio.

> The captain of the rangers
> came up close to Silvano,
> and in a few seconds
> Silvano Garcia was dead.

Similar attitudes are expressed on the Sonora-Arizona border, for example, when the hard-case hero of "El Corrido de Cananea" is made to say:

> Me agarraon los cherifes
> al estilo americano,

como al hombre de delito,
todos con pistola en mano.

The sheriffs caught me
in the American style,
as they would a wanted man,
all of them pistol in hand.

The partition of Nuevo Santander was also to have political effects, arising from the strong feeling among the lower Rio Grande people that the land on both sides of the river was equally theirs. This involved feelings on a very local and personal level, rather than the rhetoric of national politics, and is an attitude occasionally exhibited by some old Rio Grande people to this day. Driving north along one of today's highways toward San Antonio, Austin, or Houston, they are likely to say as the highway crosses the Nueces, "We are now entering Texas." Said in jest, of course, but the jest has its point. Unlike Mexicans in California, New Mexico, and the old colony of Texas, the Rio Grande people experienced the dismemberment of México in a very immediate way. So the attitude developed, early and naturally, that a border Mexican was "en su sierra" in Texas even if he had been born in Tamaulipas. Such feelings, of course, were the basis for the revolts of Cortina and Pizana. They reinforced the borderer's disregard of political and social boundaries. And they led in a direct line to the Chicano movement and its mythic concept of Aztlan. For the Chicano does not base his claim to the Southwest on royal land grants or on a lineage that goes back to the Spanish "conquistadores." On the contrary, he is more likely to be the child or grandchild of immigrants. He bases his claim to Aztlan on his Mexican culture and his "mestizo" heritage.

Conversely, the Texas-born Mexican continued to think of México as "our land" also. That this at times led to problems of identity is seen in the folksongs of the border. In 1885, for example, Rito Garcia protests illegal police entry into his home by shooting a few officers of Cameron County, Texas. He makes it across the river and feels safe, unaware that Porfirio Diaz has an extradition agreement with the United States. Arrested and returned to Texas, according to the corrido, he expresses amazement:

Yo nunca hubiera creido
que mi país tirano fuera,

que Mainero me entrega
a la nación extranjera.

I never would have thought
that my country would be so unjust,
that Mainero would hand me over
to a foreign nation.

And he adds bitterly:

Mexicanos, no hay que fiar
en nuestra propia nación,
nunca vayan a buscar
a México protección.

Mexicans, we can put no trust
in our own nation;
never go to México
asking for protection.

But the Mexicanos to whom he gives this advice are Texas-Mexicans.

ENDNOTE

1. The uprising occurred on the lower Rio Grande border and involved a group of Texas-Mexican rancheros attempting to create a Spanish-speaking republic in South Texas. Pizana endeavored to appeal to other U.S. minority groups.

Explore

What is the Treaty of Guadalupe Hidalgo? What role did it play on the way of living on the U.S.-México border?

Collaborate

With one or two other classmates, examine border folklore. What are corridos? Do research. Identify three specific examples (poems, ballads, stories, songs, etc.) of border folklore that present smugglers as "variants of the hero of cultural conflict." Share these examples with the class. You may identify other corridos as well.

Compose

Reread the Carrasco corrido and the two from a tequilero ballad of the 30's. Select one of the three corridos and write a review of it. What is it saying? How vivid and realistic is the corridor? What is its purpose? Does it achieve its purpose? Explain your answer and evaluation of the corrido.

Gabriel Thompson is both an author and a journalist. He is the recipient of the Richard J. Margolis Award and the Studs Terkel Media Award. Thompson has written for a number of periodicals, including the New York Times and The Brooklyn Rail. As author of numerous books, including There's No José Here: Following the Hidden Lives of Mexican Immigrants and Working in the Shadows, Thompson describes the immigrant experience.

INTRODUCTION TO THERE'S NO JOSÉ HERE: FOLLOWING THE HIDDEN LIVES OF MEXICAN IMMIGRANTS

BY GABRIEL THOMPSON

IT HAPPENED OVER and over again:

"Hi, is José there?"

"Uh, there's no José here."

"Yes there is. Can you please ask someone if he's there now?"

"Let me see…ummm…I'm pretty sure we don't have a José."

"Do me a favor, just ask."

"Fine." Getting agitated now. "Hold on a second." Several minutes pass:

"Hello?"

"Hola, José, soy yo, Gabriel."

"Hola, Gabriel. ¿Qué onda?"

My friend José, from the southern México state of Puebla, has worked for eight years at a Manhattan company that produces low-end jewelry. Still, whenever I called him at work, I was told he wasn't there. I'd have to insist that whoever answered the phone inquire into the existence of a José in their shop. Eventually, they would discover that—lo and behold—a José did indeed work at their company, and had in fact put in more than twenty-four thousand irretrievable hours of his life laboring for their benefit. The first few times this occurred I made a note of it. After half a dozen identical interactions, I stopped keeping track.

Minuteman Volunteer Flyer

In April of 2005 a group calling itself the Minutemen made international news when they gathered approximately 150 people on the U.S.-México border and sat on lawn chairs looking through binoculars into the empty desert. *I spent a week living with them on the campus of a bible college, which the Minutemen quickly attempted to turn into a military compound. By the second day they had rechristened the church cafeteria as the "mess hall," and the grounds were transformed into the "perimeter." The volunteers were white, mostly men but also a good number of women (who nonetheless insisted on being called Minutemen), and all of them were angry.

My main desire, reporting on their activities at the time for an online news magazine, was to discover what it was that they were so angry about. They were small in number, for sure, but one couldn't dismiss their dedication. All had decided to take time out from their normal lives to trek to Arizona. Some came from as far away as New York, as I did—paying their own way to live in primitive conditions and face sunburns and scorpions. Why?

They were mostly angry about abstractions and generalizations: Mexicans refused to learn English. They were lazy and came to the United States to get on welfare. Or else they came to the States to steal jobs from U.S. citizens. They were drug dealers. Violent. Disease spreaders. Child molesters. Immoral.

I wasn't interested in battling abstraction against abstraction. Instead, I asked the same question over and over again: "Do you actually know any Mexican immigrants?" Although one wouldn't expect any of the Minutemen to have attempted to make serious relational inroads in the Mexican community, most were from the immigrant-heavy state of California. Surely a few of them had some sort of contact with Mexicans, or so I figured. Yet each volunteer I spoke with drew a blank; none knew any Mexican immigrants personally. There was a battle raging over Mexican immigrants, but the Mexican immigrants themselves were somehow ignored, like my friend José at the jewelry factory. At the same time, they were regularly referred to, but as an abstraction, like the many "Josés" at the construction company.

The problem is, politically charged abstractions don't necessarily tell us anything useful. Though I don't personally know any Mexican immigrants who are drug dealers or child molesters, they undoubtedly exist. The same can be said about born-again Christians, police officers, Boy Scout leaders, surgeons, lifelong Chevy drivers, and residents of Arkansas.

Abstractions are ultimately dehumanizing, and in the U.S. debate over how to handle the "problem" of Mexican immigrants, the competing narratives crashing up against one another remain at arm's length from the immigrants themselves. Americans are so busy catapulting statistics at one another, fighting tooth and nail over the "goodness" or "badness" of Mexican immigrants (and, for that matter, nonwhite immigrants in general) that immigrants get buried under the deluge, their voices suffocated beneath a mountain of footnotes and policy papers.

There are two general perspectives of immigrants. The first view, shared by mostly conservative whites, and perhaps best exemplified by the Minutemen participants, is of immigrants as lawbreakers, as moral degenerates who present a clear and ever-growing threat to what is referred to as our "way of life," in itself another abstract notion that is rarely actually explained. People within this camp usually have a glorified notion of a pristine past, where things were somehow better (in practical terms, sometimes all this means is that one didn't have to overhear conversations in Spanish while purchasing groceries). Throw in the so-called War on Terror, and such people suddenly have another reason to fear, and loathe, immigrants. In our country, there is a long tradition of nativism, and that tradition persists today.

The second, more sympathetic view is of immigrants as innocent and exploited victims, as a nameless mass of misery. According to this caricature, immigrants are honorable, hardworking people who come to the United States in order to better their lives but are taken advantage of because of an unjust social order. They are humble, thankful, grateful. Simple folk. Again, though more sympathetic than the conservative caricature, this view simplifies the immigrant reality and is ultimately condescending. Throughout the history of the United States, immigrants have suffered special exploitations, of course, but they have also been among our most dedicated fighters for social justice. They are not passive and they are not resigned—at least no more than any of us. To treat them as a perfect people is ridiculous. To pretend that things simply happen to them, that they naturally assume the mantle of victimhood, is as inaccurate as to pretend that they are more prone to lawbreaking than U.S. citizens. Call my friend Enrique a victim, and he will laugh in your face; call him an asshole, and he'll nod and say, "You're right, but so are you." Mexican immigrants fall somewhere between angels and assholes—again, as we all do.

My own journey into the world of Mexican immigrants came about as most life-altering developments do: by pure chance. After graduating from college in California I moved to Brooklyn to work as a community organizer. The primary focus was tackling the problems of low-income tenants living in poor housing or facing eviction. It quickly became obvious that the people living in the worst housing conditions, and who felt least comfortable taking action, were the Mexican immigrants.

My closest Mexican friend soon became a man named Enrique. This book is largely his story. As his adventures in Brooklyn progressed, I got to know his wife, his children, his parents, his friends, his uncles, his cousins, his nieces, and his nephews. I should state here that this book has been made possible only through the openness and patience of Enrique, who was forced to suffer through thousands of my questions—often inane, as he liked to correctly complain—and who welcomed me with open arms into his life. With him I attended court dates, funerals, weddings and births. I traveled with him by car from Brooklyn to his hometown in southern México, and to Fort Bragg military base to say good-bye to his best friend, who was being deployed to Iraq. At times Enrique and I drove each other a bit crazy—long, sleepless road trips will do that—but still, whatever he was going through, he wouldn't fail to call, and his message always the same: *"Güero,"* he would begin—white boy, my unofficial nickname—"You've got to come along with me if you really want to be able to understand what it's like to be an immigrant." And we would be off—sometimes to housing court, sometimes to a celebration of some sort, sometimes just to eat a large meal of beans, rice, and tortillas while bullshitting for an hour or two. This book, then, is not an authoritative study of Mexican immigrants; this is not a book that says *Here is what Mexicans are like.* My goal is more modest, more focused. I am telling the story of several friendships, several hardships, several interesting lives.

To err on the side of caution, most of the immigrants in this book are identified by their first names only. I don't know if the Department of Homeland Security would attempt to track down the people within these pages who are living in the country illegally. Probably not; I would hope the department has better things to do. Either way, I don't care to find out. In addition, for privacy reasons several characters are given pseudonyms, and when this occurs I make a note of it.

Finally, a note on terminology: Labels can be politically explosive, as one quickly learns when writing about Mexican immigrants who are in the United States illegally. On one side are the people—overwhelmingly Anglo—who prefer to call such people "illegal aliens" or even "invaders." These labels, often purposefully, conjure up imaged of exotic outsiders who are subversive and have criminal tendencies. A more succinct variation of the term "illegal immigrants" is simply "illegals." This, too, is dehumanizing, boiling down an existence to one of illegitimacy. Someone who drives without a license is breaking the law, but we don't call that person an "illegal" driver, and we would never think of shortening this label to an "illegal." In my book, the same should go for immigrant status.

One evening while watching the news I saw a white man shouting, "Go home, illegals!" at a group of immigrants who were demonstrating for their right to have driver's licenses. As the camera panned the crowd of protesters I could see many broad Indian faces, faces that are indigenous to the continent we all share. The irony was lost on the red-faced Anglo, whose ancestors grew up thousands of miles away.

Partly in sympathy with my Mexican friends, partly in wishing to disassociate myself from the red-faced Anglo, I choose not to use the term "illegal" in this book, except when quoting others. The truth is the vast majority of the immigrants I know in New York City, including Enrique, are descendents of the Mixtec, one of the major pre-Columbian civilizations in the Americas. Their indigenous blood runs deep.

I once saw an old Latino man wearing a T-shirt that read "Who's the Illegal, Pilgrim?" The man has a point, and in this book I refer to the

Mexican immigrants who are here without the blessing of the United States government as *undocumented*. Hopefully, this book will play a modest role in their documentation.

NOTES

1. Though news reports usually echoed the Minutemen's claim that "thousands" of volunteers had shown up, by my own estimation—and according to the only newspaper that actually bothered to count—roughly 150 participants came, and this number was cut in half several days into the project.

According to Thompson, what are the two general perspectives of immigrants? Do you agree with him? Why or why not?

In a small group, discuss who the Minutemen are. What is their purpose? What is their position? Do you support this position? Why or why not? Discuss these questions and the impact your answers have on immigration.

Thompson states, "Abstractions are ultimately dehumanizing." What does he mean by this? How does this statement relate to Mexican immigrants? In an essay, explain your view on this statement. Consider the two perspectives on immigrants that Thompson believes exist in American society. Explain your perspective and relate it to your personal experience.

Arian Campo-Flores has been Miami Bureau Chief for Newsweek *magazine since 2002. As a writer for* Newsweek, *Campo-Flores, in this article, presents the fallacies in believing that immigrants hurt the U.S. economy.*

WHY AMERICANS THINK (WRONGLY) THAT ILLEGAL IMMIGRANTS HURT THE ECONOMY

BY ARIAN CAMPO-FLORES

At the heart of the debate over illegal immigration lies one key question: are immigrants good or bad for the economy? The American public overwhelmingly thinks they're bad. In a recent *New York Times*/CBS News poll, 74 percent of respondents said illegal immigrants weakened the economy, compared to only 17 percent who said they strengthened it. Yet the consensus among most economists is that immigration, both legal and illegal, provides a small net boost to the economy. Immigrants provide cheap labor, lower the prices of everything from produce to new homes, and leave consumers with a little more money in their pockets. They also replenish—and help fund benefits for—an aging American labor force that will retire in huge numbers over the next few decades. Also, an increase in the number of American workers is needed to prevent the U.S. from having too few working-age adults to pay for retiree benefits in a few decades, as many European nations currently do. So why is there such a discrepancy between the perception of immigrants' impact on the economy and the reality?

There are a number of familiar theories. Some point to the ravages of the Great Recession, arguing that people are anxious and feel threatened by an influx of new workers (though anti-immigrant sentiment ran high at times prior to the crash of 2008). Others highlight the strain that undocumented immigrants place on public services, like schools, hospitals, and jails. Still others emphasize the role of race, arguing that foreigners provide a convenient repository for the nation's fears and insecurities. There's some truth to all of these explanations, but they aren't quite sufficient.

To get a better understanding of what's going on, consider the way immigration's impact is felt. Though its overall effect may be positive, its costs and benefits are distributed unevenly. David Card, an economist at the University of California, Berkeley notes that the ones who profit most directly from immigrants' low-cost labor are businesses and employers—meatpacking plants in Nebraska, for instance, or agribusinesses in California's Central Valley. Granted, these producers' savings probably translate into lower prices at the grocery store, but how many consumers make that mental connection at the checkout counter? As for the drawbacks of illegal immigration, these, too, are concentrated. Native low-skilled workers suffer most from the competition of foreign labor. According to a study by George Borjas, a Harvard economist, immigration reduced the wages of American high-school dropouts by 9 percent between 1980 and 2000. Not surprisingly, surveys show that those without a high-school diploma tend to oppose illegal immigration most fervently.

There's another distortion in the way immigration's costs and benefits are parceled out. Many undocumented workers pay money to the federal government, in the form of Social Security contributions and income taxes, and take less in return, says Gordon Hanson, an economist at the University of California, San Diego. At the state and local levels, however, it's a different story. There, illegal immigrants also make contributions, through property and sales taxes, but on balance, they use more in public services, such as schools, health benefits, and welfare assistance. As a result, says Hanson, the federal government ends up with a net gain in its coffers, while "states get stuck with the bill."

This breeds resentment among taxpayers. In a 2005 paper, Hanson analyzed how the size of the undocumented population and its use of public assistance affected attitudes toward immigration. He found that among low-skilled workers, opposition to immigration stemmed mainly from the competitive threat posed by the newcomers. Among high-skilled, better-educated employees, however, opposition was strongest in states with both high numbers of immigrants and relatively generous social services. What worried them most, in other words, was the fiscal burden of immigration. That conclusion was reinforced by another finding: that their opposition appeared to soften when that fiscal burden decreased, as occurred with welfare reform in the 1990s, which curbed immigrants' access to certain benefits.

Beyond these economic rationales for anti-immigrant views, there's a demographic one as well. Illegal immigrants used to be clustered in a handful of big states, like California, Texas, and New York. But in the 1990s, they began dispersing en masse, chasing jobs in the remote reaches of the country. As a result, California's share of the undocumented population dropped from 42 percent in 1990 to 22 percent in 2008, according to the Pew Hispanic Center. A group of 28 fast-growing states, such as North Carolina and Georgia, more than doubled their share, from 14 percent in 1990 to 32 percent in 2008. Natives in those areas had barely any experience with undocumented immigrants, and they felt overwhelmed by the sudden change. The once distant debate over illegal immigration was now bubbling up in the heart of their communities.

In a new book, *Brokered Boundaries*, Douglas Massey and Magaly Sánchez cite research showing that such rapid demographic change tends to trigger anti-immigrant sentiment when it gets entangled in inflammatory political rhetoric. They argue that in the past several decades, a "Latino threat narrative" has come to dominate political and media discourse. In the 1980s, President Ronald Reagan began framing immigration as an issue of "national security," they write. In the 1990s, the image of the immigrant-as-freeloader gained wide circulation. And in the 2000s, there was Lou Dobbs, railing against an "invasion of illegal aliens" that waged "war on the middle class." "The majority of Americans are more ambivalent than hostile [to undocumented immigration]," says Massey, a professor at Princeton. But "the hostile part can be mobilized from time to time," by what he calls "anti-immigrant entrepreneurs."

The irony is that for all the overexcited debate, the net effect of immigration is minimal (about a one tenth of 1 percent gain in gross domestic product, according to Hanson). Even for those most acutely affected—say, low-skilled workers, or California residents—the impact isn't all that dramatic. "The shrill voices have tended to dominate our perceptions," says Daniel Tichenor, a political science professor at the University of Oregon. "But when all those factors are put together and the economists crunch the numbers, it ends up being a net positive, but a small one." Too bad most people don't realize it.

Explore

What is xenophobia? What role does it play on the issue of immigration?

Invent

Create a list of ways illegal immigrants hurt the U.S. economy. Create another list of ways illegal immigrants help the U.S. economy.

Compose

Write an essay, fully supported with evidence of your choice (personal experience, examples, credible sources, statistics, etc.), where you take either position: Illegal immigrants *hurt* the U.S. economy or illegal immigrants *help* the U.S. economy.

Johanna Ferreira is a freelance writer and editorial assistant for the City University of New York (CUNY). She has written for periodicals, such as Latina and SELF magazines. In this article, Ferreira describes legendary guitarist Carlos Santana's speech against Georgia's and Arizona's new immigration laws. Santana spoke to the audience during the Atlanta Braves' fifth annual Civil Rights Game as he was given the Beacon Change Award.

CARLOS SANTANA SPEAKS OUT AGAINST IMMIGRATION LAWS IN ARIZONA, GEORGIA

BY JOHANNA FERREIRA

On Sunday, legendary guitar god Carlos Santana was given the Beacon of Change award before the Atlanta Braves played their fifth annual Civil Rights Game.

Musician, Carlos Santana

Santana used the opportunity to stand up for immigrants and against the new Georgia and Arizona immigration laws. "The people of Arizona and the people of Atlanta, Georgia, you should be ashamed of yourselves," he said. Although some people in the crowd began to boo at Santana for his statement, he continued in a press conference after the game, "This law is not correct. It's a cruel law, actually, This is about fear. Stop shucking and jiving. People are afraid we're going to steal your job. No we aren't. You're not going to change sheets and clean toilets. I would invite all Latin people to do nothing for about two weeks so you can see who really, really is running the economy. Who cleans the sheets? Who cleans the toilets? Who babysits? I am here to give voice to the invisible."

On Friday, only two days before the ceremony, Georgia Governor Nathan Deal signed HR 70, a bill almost identical to the Arizona SB 1070 law. The bill gives the state and local police the power to demand immigration documentation from any Latinos they suspect to be undocumented. It also requires that employers check the immigration status of any new hires.

Santana, who immigrated to San Francisco from México back in the 1960s, concluded: "This is the United States. This is the land of the free. If people want the immigration laws to keep passing, then everybody should get out and leave the American Indians here."

Explore

Research both Georgia's new bill, HR 70, and Arizona's new law, SB 1070. How are they similar? How are they different?

Invent

Who is Carlos Santana? How strong of a voice is he for Latinos(as)? Is he a credible and persuasive spokesperson on immigration? Why or why not?

Collaborate

In a small group discussion, determine whether Santana chose the right time and place (kairos) to express his view on immigration and Georgia's and Arizona's new immigration bill and law.

Compose

What kind of role or influence does and can the music industry have on immigration reform? What about Hollywood? Can actors and directors influence immigration reform? In an essay, take a stand on whether Hollywood and/or the music industry can or cannot influence immigration reform. Explain your answers. Give examples. Support your arguments.

Fox News Latino features news, politics, entertainment, health, and life style stories that affect the Latino community. It also offers a site for Spanish news and features in English from Spanish speaking countries.

OBAMA HOSTS BIPARTISAN MEETING OF IMMIGRATION REFORM SUPPORTERS

By Fox News Latino

President Barack Obama has called upon a bipartisan group of immigration reform supporters, that includes Republican California Gov. Arnold Schwarzenegger and New York Mayor Michael Bloomberg, to discuss the importance of fixing the nation's "broken immigration system."

The invitees are expected to meet with Obama at the White House on Tuesday afternoon in an attempt to show wide and varied support for revamping the immigration system.

Besides Schwarzenegger, New York Mayor Michael Bloomberg, San Antonio Mayor Julian Castro and Philadelphia Police Commissioner Charles Ramsey, who also served as Washington, D.C., police chief, are among those invited.

In a statement issued late Monday, the White House said the president is holding the meeting to discuss the importance of fixing the nation's immigration system to meet the country's 21st century economic and national security needs.

The White House said business and religious leaders, as well as current and former public officials from across the political spectrum were to be invited. The statement was attributed to a White House senior official who was not further identified.

In a Monday afternoon interview with Dallas television station WFAA, Obama underscored the need for bilateral support to set new immigration policy.

"The question is going to be, are we going to be able to find some Republicans who can partner with me and others to get this done once and for all instead of using it as a political football," he said.

Obama has been under fire from Latino and immigration activists and Spanish-language media for failing to take up immigration in his first term. He has been consistently reminded of his campaign promise to address immigration early in his administration.

Although Obama has repeatedly said he is committed to immigration overhaul, the deportation of a record 393,000 immigrants last year and other enforcement tactics during his administration have drawn criticism in the immigrant and Hispanic communities.

Over the weekend, Illinois Democratic Rep. Luis Gutiérrez, who helped rally Hispanic voters to support Obama during the 2008 campaign, told a Chicago crowd he was not sure he could back Obama in 2012 if the president did not step up immigration changes. Last week, 22 Senate Democrats sent a letter to Obama asking him to delay deportations of young undocumented immigrants who were brought into the country by their parents.

Explore

Who are the invitees to Obama's meeting on revamping the immigration system? What role does each play in immigration reform?

Collaborate

In a small group, evaluate Obama's guest list. Who should be invited to this discussion? How would this person contribute productively to the discussion on immigration reform?

Compose

In an essay, select one individual who should be invited to President Obama's meeting on immigration reform. Why should this person be invited? What role does this individual play in immigration reform and system? This individual may be someone famous or an everyday person you know. He/she can be a local, national, or international entity, but the person must be living. Be sure to introduce this individual with all his/her credentials in your essay. Justify your selection and support your reasons for having this person be Obama's guest to the discussion on the immigration system and reform.

MAJOR ASSIGNMENTS

MAJOR ASSIGNMENT #1
WRITING *ABOUT* THE COMMUNITY
AN INFORMATIVE ESSAY
A SERVICE-LEARNING PROJECT

BACKGROUND

Service-learning is a teaching method that allows students to practice what they are learning in the classroom in a real workplace setting, more specifically with a community non-profit organization. Students in a writing course doing a service-learning project can, as scholar Thomas Deans explains, "write *for, about,* or *with* the community." This assignment, along with the following major assignments #2 and #3, asks you to work with a non-profit organization where you will practice different genres of writing.

BENEFITS OF SERVICE-LEARNING

Because service-learning allows you to go beyond the classroom when you write, you may practice writing to different audiences and for different purposes. Service-learning also gives you work experience and allows you to network with professionals. Other readers, besides your writing instructor, may give you feedback on your writing and literacy skills. In addition, service-learning provides you with the opportunity to become civically engaged and learn more about your community and its needs. You are also building a bridge between the community and your university or college.

ASSIGNMENT

You will write an informative essay describing a community non-profit organization related to immigration and/or border issues. You will volunteer a specific number of hours, designated by your writing instructor, at this agency. As you work there, you must familiarize yourself with the organization's mission, objectives, clients, accomplishments, and needs. Your purpose for this informative essay is to inform your writing instructor and your classmates of this organization's goal and how it contributes to the well-being of the community and its residents.

CHOOSING A NON-PROFIT ORGANIZATION

The main requirement in selecting a non-profit organization is that it must relate to immigration and/or border issues of some sort, whether it is cultural, linguistic, economic, political, etc. Consider the location of the agency. Also, you will need to find out if they allow student volunteers and if you are required to be there for your tasks or whether you will be performing tasks that can be done from your home. Make sure you clarify that this is for a college writing course and that you will be writing an essay about their organization. You must also identify who will be supervising your work.

Again, immigration and/or border issues must be the guiding point to your selection. For example, in El Paso, Texas, several immigration and border non-profit organizations exist, including:

- Las Americas Immigrant Advocacy Center
- Diocesan Migrant and Refugee Services
- AVANCE
- Mujer Obrera
- Border Network for Human Rights
- Sin Fronteras
- Project Puente
- Centro Mujeres de la Esperanza
- Project Bravo
- The U.S.-México Border Philanthropy Partnership
- U.S.-México Border Health Commission
- Border Environment Cooperation Commission (BECC)

You should also look into local parishes; they, many times, have community ministries that serve immigrants or address border issues.

RESEARCH

Go to the non-profit organization's website. Visit the organization. Interview the director, key personnel, and/or clients being served by the non-profit organization. Talk to people. Search for articles on the organization. Look at local periodicals, such as the local newspaper, local city magazine, and even the local Business Bureau. Perhaps your university or college campus has a service-learning office or center for civic engagement where you can find more information on the agency.

REMINDER

Volunteering and service-learning are not just a matter of showing up at the agency and asking to work there. You must allow yourself sufficient time to contact, visit, and negotiate projects and tasks with the key person at the non-profit organization. At times, the agency may have specific requirements for the student learner/volunteer, such as immunizations, a background check, and/or training or an orientation. You may also create a *contract* with the agency and your instructor where you list the specific duties, tasks, and time commitment you will be giving to the agency.

MAJOR ASSIGNMENT #2
WRITING *FOR* THE COMMUNITY
CREATING A COMMUNITY TEXT
A SERVICE-LEARNING PROJECT

BACKGROUND

Now that you have learned about a specific non-profit organization relating to immigration and/or borders, it is time to write *for* them (Refer to Major Assignments #1 and #3). When you write *for* the community, you will deal more with workplace discourse, not so much academic discourse. In other words, you must produce needed writing or communication products for the agencies, such as proposals, business correspondence, grants, newsletters, manuals, and pamphlets. Your first step should be to identify what your non-profit agency's literacy needs are and then evaluate your literacy skills to see if you are qualified to produce the necessary texts.

ASSIGNMENT

When you meet with your agency supervisor (mentor), you must negotiate what document(s) you will produce by a specific deadline (established by your instructor and agency mentor). Based on the agency's needs and resources, you will produce at least one community text. Possibilities include creating or contributing to the non-profit organization's newsletter, producing a pamphlet or brochure for them, developing or revising the agency's website, and/or identifying and writing a grant proposal for the non-profit organization. Your instructor must approve your proposed text(s), and you must establish a schedule for the text(s) to be completed. In addition, your proposed community text may require you to do research, conduct interviews, attend meetings, etc.

ABOUT CONTRACTS

In creating a contract between you, the agency mentor, and your instructor, you must list all contact information for all three parties. You must identify and clearly explain each text and tasks that you will be completing by either the end of the semester or the specified date (established by either or both your instructor and the agency mentor). Only list tasks and products that you will be able to complete within the time frame you are allowed. This contract must be signed by all three parties: agency mentor, your instructor, and you.

REMINDER

If the task(s) and end product(s) require you to use other languages besides English, you must be at least proficient in the other language, and your instructor must give you her/his approval. On the El Paso-Juárez border, Spanish is the dominant language in close to 70% of the households. Thus, most community texts are produced in both English and Spanish. Add to this that Spanish on the border is a variety of Spanish; it is border Spanish and even border English— dialects typical of the El Paso-Juárez border.

MAJOR ASSIGNMENT #3
KEEPING A SERVICE-LEARNING JOURNAL AND
WRITING A REFLECTIVE ESSAY

BACKGROUND

You have researched and are becoming familiar with a non-profit organization relating to immigration and/or borders. Refer to Assignments #1 and #2. You are working with the agency and helping them produce a text(s). As you serve and learn during this experience, it is important for you to record your progress, impressions, accomplishments, and concerns. *Reflection* is a key component of service-learning. Reflection also allows you to attain critical awareness of your community's needs.

ASSIGNMENT

Your assignment consists of two different texts. You will be keeping a service-learning journal from the day you meet with the agency you will be working with, and at the end, you will write a reflection essay on your service-learning experience to be read by your writing instructor.

Keeping a Service-Learning Journal

You may choose the format for your service-learning journal. However, you must do the following:

- Provide the date and time spent on your service-learning text/tasks for each journal entry.
- Provide an entry for every time you visit the agency, work at home, on campus, or any other site on the text/tasks for your non-profit organization. This includes work done on-line, phone conversations, meetings, trainings, etc.
- Label each entry clearly: date, time, location, and work done. Be specific in describing what you did and what you accomplished that day.
- Reflect and analyze your work, your observations, your conversations, and interactions with others at the agency.
- Consider and discuss any concerns, obstacles, or problems you faced while working with the non-profit on that day and time.
- Share your accomplishments and feedback you received from others at the agency.

- Connect what you are doing for the agency with your writing course and/or studies.

Organization, genuine reflection, and critical analysis must be evident in your journal and its entries.

Writing a Reflection Essay

Once you have ended your service-learning project, you will write a reflection essay. Your intended reader for this essay is your writing instructor and classmates. Your intended purpose is to inform, reflect, and make connections between what you did for the non-profit organization and your writing course objectives and/or your general studies or intended major. Follow these guidelines:

- Write an introduction (with a thesis, a guiding idea), a body (multiple paragraphs), and a conclusion.
- Provide a brief overview of your non-profit organization and your contract, specifying what tasks and text(s) you committed yourself to completing for the agency.
- Explain what, if any, connections you were able to make between your service-learning experience and your studies/writing course.
- Discuss specific ways this service-learning experience affected you: academically, professionally, civically, personally, etc.
- Identify one word or phrase that describes your overall service-learning experience. Explain why and how this one word or phrase gives a true image or picture to the reader of your service and learning.
- Revise, edit, and proofread your essay before you submit it to your instructor. Attach your service-learning journal to this reflection essay.

MAJOR ASSIGNMENT #4
WRITING A LETTER TO A LAW OR POLICY MAKER OR POLITICIAN

BACKGROUND

Consider your position on immigration. Where do you stand on immigration reform? What would you like for your city, state, or the nation and its government to do for immigrants and its borders? Select a city, state, or national politician, law or policy maker. For example, you read the debate between Arizona Governor Jan Brewer and New Mexico Governor Bill Richardson. Do you agree with either of their views? What kind of immigration reform would you like to take place? Or should there be no immigration reform?

ASSIGNMENT

Write a letter to your state governor, senator, or representative. You may also choose to write to the local mayor or city council. Your choice will depend on the purpose of the letter you will be writing. If your proposed course of action is at the city level, then your intended audience should be at the local level. If your proposed course of action is at the national level, your intended audience should be at the state or national level. Your proposal and purpose will determine your audience.

RESEARCH

Use this book's readings and use newspapers, magazines, and websites to research the various aspects and issues involved in the debate over immigration, including illegal immigrants and their status in the U.S. You can also conduct field research, such as interviews and surveys.

ESTABLISH YOUR ARGUMENTS

Write summary statements of the different key arguments on immigration. Identify the ones you support. Compose a recommendation(s) on a specific issue, argument, need, or problem relating to immigration/border security. Explain your argument(s), support it with evidence, and provide and explain, in detail, your proposed recommendation(s) to the intended reader.

ABOUT LETTERS

Be sure to have an inside address (address of the reader) and provide a return address (your address). Begin with a salutation (a greeting), write the content of your letter in multiple paragraphs, and end with a closing (ex. Sincerely, ...). Be polite and use the appropriate tone for your letter (serious, caring, formal, etc.). Single-space within paragraphs; double-space between paragraphs. Make sure you edit and proofread your letter before submitting it to your intended reader.

MAJOR ASSIGNMENT #5
ANALYZING WEBSITES ON IMMIGRATION

BACKGROUND

Different media and communication means exist for individuals to convey their messages and inform the public. Because immigration and border issues are important topics for cities, states, and countries, conveying information is crucial. Websites abound, but are they all credible and effective in addressing the various issues on immigration and borders? If you want to be accurately informed, you must analyze and evaluate these different sources of information.

ASSIGNMENT

Write an evaluation essay in which you analyze and compare the ways that two different websites address the issue of immigration and/or borders. Evaluate both sites. Examine the content, purpose, intended audience, and rhetorical strategies each of these two websites uses to persuade its audience. Make sure that in your essay you take a clear position evaluating both websites and that you provide evidence from each website to support your analysis.

RESEARCH

Go to the following website:

imym.org/immigrationintervisitationproject/
imymintervisitationimmigration/ sourcesinfoimmigration/view

This site provides a list of sources on immigration and border concerns. In addition, it breaks it down to subtopics and provides websites on the different aspects of immigration and border issues. You may refer to other websites of your choice.

INVENTION

In analyzing websites, consider the following questions:

1. What is the purpose of the website?
2. Whom is the website addressing?
3. How is the website appealing to its audience? Through their emotions, logic, or by establishing credibility by its name, its duration on-line, its

content, authors, etc.? In other words, is the website appealing to you through what Greek philosopher Aristotle identifies as pathos, logos, and/or ethos?

4. How credible is the website? What makes it credible or suspicious?

5. What message are the website's content, visuals, language, and organization conveying to its audience?

6. Does the website suggest a course of action? If so, what action is this?

ABOUT EVALUATION ESSAYS

Evaluation essays identify key criteria for their analysis. For example, you may choose content, purpose, visuals, and organization as your criteria for evaluating the two websites. You may come up with your own criteria, but whatever they are, you must use the same factors for both websites. The main idea of your essay, the thesis statement, should be the position you are taking in your evaluation. You may opt to convince the reader of how one website is more credible and/or useful than the other. In short, for evaluation essays to be successful, you must establish criteria, provide a thesis statement, and support your arguments with specific examples and evidence.

MAJOR ASSIGNMENT #6
CREATING A FAMILY TREE AND WRITING PROFILES

BACKGROUND

Knowing your roots and heritage is important to your identity. Though you may know who your immediate family is, identifying your extended family can be helpful. Even going beyond your extended family, investigating the origins of your family can give you insight on who you are and where you came from. You may not know whose blood you carry and what lands your ancestors have visited or are originally from. Family trees provide you with a venue to learn your ancestry and roots.

ASSIGNMENT—CREATING A FAMILY TREE

Construct a family tree or genealogical chart. Research through family interviews, ancestry websites, and other sources your family background. Be sure to show through your family tree or genealogical chart the relationships, locations, and movements of family members. Once your family tree or chart is completed, post or place it in a prominent place in the classroom. Share with the class what you have learned by completing this activity.

RESEARCH

Investigate how members on your family tree or genealogical chart relocated from one region/country to another. Establish how many, if any, of your family members migrated to America. If any of these family members, perhaps grandparents or even parents, are immigrants to America, investigate the circumstances they faced and how they coped with these circumstances. Personal interviews with family members will help you gather this information.

ASSIGNMENT—WRITING A PROFILE

After you have constructed your family tree or chart and you have researched your family background, select one specific family member that intrigues or stands out to you. If possible, conduct an interview with this relative. Do research on this family member. Write a profile of this individual.

INVENTION

Why does this person intrigue or stand out to you? What is your relationship to this person? Did you, before doing this assignment, know this person and your relationship to him/her? Identify personal characteristics and life events of this individual. How does this person symbolize borders or immigration for you?

MAJOR ASSIGNMENT #7
CREATING AND HOLDING A BORDER CULTURE FAIR

BACKGROUND

As you discover how different borders exist in any society, you should begin forming a definition for "border." It is important for communities to identify and recognize the different borders existing in their lives. Just as the El Paso, Texas-Juárez, México border has come to be known as "the border or the borderlands," it has also created its own "border culture." This culture can be seen through its language, art, literature, music, customs, entertainment, food, jobs, money, sports, life styles, economy, crafts, holidays, family life, clothing, theater, education, religions, manners, housing, stories, legends, television, and even the status of women, elders, and children.

ASSIGNMENT

As a class, you will hold a *border culture fair* on campus. Your purpose is to make students, faculty, staff, and the community recognize and/or value the different borders existing within your community. You can have poster exhibits, booths, workshops, activities, and guest speakers and performers.

QUESTIONS ON LOGISTICS

Consider these questions as the starting point for the border culture fair:

- When should you hold the fair? What day? What time?
- Where is the best location for the fair? On or off campus?
- How will you set up for the fair?
- Whose permission do you need to be able to hold the fair at the selected location?
- How will you advertise the fair?

QUESTIONS ON ORGANIZATION

Consider the following questions to help you organize and complete the necessary tasks:

- How will tasks and responsibilities be assigned?
- Is it more effective to have each student work independently or collaboratively in teams?

- Who will set up for the fair?
- Who will clean up?
- Which specific activities do you want to have at the fair?
- Who should be invited to the fair?
- What booths and workshops should be provided at the fair?
- Who is going to head each event and activity at the fair?

Be sure to create a **schedule of events** and a **map identifying each exhibit, booth, and event.**

SUGGESTIONS FOR THE FAIR

Consider the following list as ideas for your border culture fair. You may come up with your own unique ideas. Brainstorm as a class.

- Invite local artists to exhibit their work.
- Invite local performers (musicians, dancers, singers, etc.) to perform.
- Invite local craft artists to give workshops and/or to sell their arts and crafts.
- Set up food booths – food unique to your border culture.
- Have a fashion show – modeling different costumes/clothes typical of your border culture.
- Have poster exhibits or booths illustrating the history, language, customs, and education of your border culture.
- Set up game booths – games related to your border culture. For example, *la loteria* is a common game on the El Paso-Juárez border.
- Invite community civil rights, human rights, or immigration leaders or advocates to speak at the fair.
- Invite local authors to speak at the fair.

ADVICE

Invite other classes to join you in creating and holding the fair. These could be other writing classes or classes in other disciplines, such as in history, sociology, languages, art, music, communication, and health. Be sure to distribute tasks equally and specifically. Work collaboratively and clarify what each student/ team of students is responsible for in order to make the border culture fair a success.

OR you may opt to do this fair on a smaller scale. Your instructor may prefer to just hold a border culture fair in your classroom. In this case, each student/team of students is responsible for a booth, exhibit, or activity.

A REMINDER

This project should be planned early in the semester to ensure guest speakers' and exhibitors' commitment for the specific time and day selected for the fair.

FILMOGRAPHY

DVD'S (FILMS AND MOVIES)

The Other Side of Immigration – Roy Germano
Mojados – Through the Night (2005)
Island of Hope, Island of Tears: The Story of Ellis Island and the American Immigration Experience (1989)
Border War: The Battle over Illegal Immigration (2006)
Dying to Get In – Brett Tolley
Crossing Arizona: Where Do You Draw the Line (2006)
De Nadie [Border Crossing]
7 Soles: Cuando Crees que el Futuro Está del Otro Lado
Sin Nombre (2009)
Innocent Voices (2007)
Under the Same Moon (2007)
Spanglish (2005)
Border: The Divide between the American Dream and the American Nightmare
Cries from the Border
South of the Border (2009)
The New Americans – Kartemquin Films (2009)
La Caminata: The Journey – New Day Films, Jamie Meltzer (2009)
The Time Has Come: An Immigrant Community Stands Up to the Border Patrol – El Paso Border Rights Coalition (2008)
A Day Without a Mexican

DOCUMENTARIES

Wetback: The Undocumented – Documentary, National Geographic, Arturo Perez Torres
The Border – Documentary, Espinosa Productions
Bracero Stories – Documentary, Cherry Lane Productions
2501 Migrants: A Journey – Reencuentros – Documentary, Cinema Libre Studio (2010)

TV SHOWS

The George Lopez Show
Ugly Betty
Lopez Tonight
Qué Pasa USA?

WORKS CITED

Anzaldúa, Gloria. *Borderlands: La Frontera*. 2nd ed. San Francisco: Aunt Lute Books, 1999. Print.

Baca, Isabel. "Exploring Diversity, Borders, and Student Identities: A Bilingual Service-Learning Workplace Writing Approach." *Reflections* VI.1 (2007): 139-50. Print.

Bañuelas, Arturo, Msgr. "Peace and Justice without Borders." Rally 29 Anapa Fence, El Paso, TX. 29 Jan. 2011. Speech.

Blakeslee, Nate. "Business as Usual." *Texas Monthly* Nov. 2010: 124-29. Print.

Brewer, Jan, Gov., and Gov. Bill Richardson. "Hard Talk: Immigration – Jan Brewer vs. Bill Richardson." *Americas Quarterly: The Policy Journal for Our Hemisphere*. Summer 2010. Web.

Campo-Flores, Arian. "Why Americans Think (Wrongly) That Illegal Immigrants Hurt the Economy." *Newsweek* 14 May 2010. Web.

Cantú, Norma E. "Living on the Border: A Wound That Will Not Heal." *Borders & Identity*. 1993. Web.

Cisneros, Sandra. From The House on Mango Street. Copyright © 1984 by Sandra Cisneros. Published by Vintage Books, a division of Random House, Inc., and in hardcover by Alfred A. Knopf in 1994. By permission of Susan Bergholz Literary Services, New York, NY and Lamy, NM. All rights reserved.

Crust, Kevin. "'A Day Without a Mexican' Is Pure Vanilla." *Los Angeles Times* 14 May 2004. Web.

Ferreira, Johanna. "Carlos Santana Speaks Out Against Immigration in Arizona, Georgia." *Latina* 17 May 2011. Web.

Garcia, Mario T. "Introduction." *Ruben Salazar: Border Correspondent*. Ed. Mario T. Garcia. Los Angeles: University of California Press, 1998. Print.

Hurwitt, Mark. "Standing Firm." *BING Images*. 3 June 2008. Web.

Luna, Sheryl. *Pity the Drowned Horses*. Notre Dame, Indiana: University of Notre Dame Press, 2005. Print.

Mintz, Steven. "Mexican American Legal Defense Fund, Myths about Immigrants." *Mexican American Voices: A Documentary Reader*. 2nd ed. United Kingdom: Wiley Blackwell, 2009. 187-190. Print.

Obama, Barack, Pres. "Remarks by the President on Comprehensive Immigration Reform." 1 July 2010. American University School of International Service, Washington, D.C. Speech.

"Obama Hosts Bipartisan Meeting of Immigration Reform Supporters." Fox News Latino. 19 April 2011. Web.

Paredes, Américo. "The Problems of Identity in a Changing Culture: Popular Expressions of Culture Conflict along the Lower Rio Grande Border." *Borders & Identity*. 1993. Web.

Ramos, Jorge. *The Other Face of America: Chronicles of the Immigrants Shaping Our Future."* Trans. Patricia J. Duncan. New York: Harper Collins Publishers, 2002. Print.

Salazar, Ruben. *Ruben Salazar: Border Correspondent.* Ed. Mario T. Garcia. Los Angeles: University of California Press, 1998. Print.

Silverstein, Jake. "Point of Border." *Texas Monthly.* Nov. 2010: 30. Print.

---. "The Immigration Dinner Party." *Texas Monthly.* Nov. 2010: 112-21. Print.

Terrazas, Beatriz. "The River That Runs through Me." *Literary El* Paso. Ed. Marcia Hatfield Daudistel . Fort Worth, Texas: Texas Christian University Press, 2009. 543-46. Print.

texasmonthly.com. Interview with Jorge Ramos. *Texas Monthly*, May 2005. Web.

Thompson, Gabriel. *There's No José Here: Following the Hidden Lives of Mexican Immigrants.* New   York: Nation Book, 2007. Print.

Vollmann, William T. "Borderlands." Rev. of *Crosses*, by Philip Caputo. *The New York Times* 15 Oct. 2009. Web.

Waslin, Michele. "Large Immigrant Populations Make Cities Safe...Just Ask El Paso." *Alternet*. 14 July 2009. Web.

BORDERS